ANTARCTIC NIGHT

Lt. Comdr.
JACK BURSEY
USCGR

ANTARCTIC NIGHT

*One Man's Story of 28,224 Hours
at the Bottom of the World*

RAND McNALLY & COMPANY
NEW YORK • CHICAGO • SAN FRANCISCO

A PATHFINDER BOOK REPRINT EDITION
Complete and Unabridged

Printed in the United States of America

ISBN: 979-8-8691-3181-2

DEDICATION

To the memory of RICHARD EVELYN BYRD, *great explorer, gallant leader and staunch friend, who first introduced me, as a lad from Newfoundland, to the Great Adventure;*

To ADA, *my dear wife, who has given complete understanding to my long love affair with Antarctica and who kept the home fire burning during my absences; and*

To MEREDITH BEYERS, *who gave my experiences form and order, and whose editorial assistance made this book possible.*

CONTENTS

Map of areas described in text, page 12

Section of photographs between pages 144–45

ANTARCTIC NIGHT

THE ENCHANTED
CONTINENT

PACIFIC OCEAN
ATLANTIC OCEAN
INDIAN OCEAN
110°
BYRD LAND
Mt. Bursey
Mt. Moulton
MARIE
HAL FLOOD MTN. RANGE
Mt. Berlin
EDSEL FORD RANGE
Byrd Station
ROCKEFELLER PLATEAU
Mt. Rea
Mt. Grace McKinley
ROCKEFELLER MOUNTAINS
150°
EDWARD VII LAND
Little America
KAINAN BAY
Little America I & III
BAY OF WHALES
DISCOVERY INLET
ROSS SEA
Support Party Mountain
ROSS ICE SHELF
QUEEN MAUD RANGE
70°
-180°
80°
85°
South Pole
BEARDMORE GLACIER
Mt. Erebus
ALEXANDER MOUNTAINS
MC MURDO SOUND
QUEEN VICTORIA LAND
ANTARCTICA
150°
110°
Legend
o-o-o-o   Dog-sled trip by Bursey, Walden, Braathen, and de Ganahl
           toward Queen Maud Range, 1929.
•-•-•-•   Dog-sled trip by Bursey, Moulton, and Berlin across Rocke-
           feller Plateau to Hal Flood Mountain, 1940.
- - - - - Mechanized reconnaissance trip by Bursey and party of Seabees
           into Marie Byrd Land, 1956.
Scale
0   60   120   180 Miles

1

WHEN I woke that morning after my first truly peaceful sleep in days, it took me a few moments to realize where I was and what I was doing there.

I was in the one place on earth which most accentuates a man's thoughts of his loved ones with acute loneliness, and I had fallen asleep dreaming that I was back home with my family. I awoke to the realization that instead, I was out on the trail in Marie Byrd Land nine thousand miles from home, five or six hundred miles from the South Pole, and some 250 miles out from Little America V, at Kainan Bay, Antarctica.

Working my way out of the sleeping bag from a cramped position, I put on my fleece-lined boots and climbed out of the cab of my weasel. No one else of the reconnaissance party was stirring. There was no sound save that of deep breathing from the men in the tent we had set up between the two sno-cats. The two men in each of the sno-cats were sleeping the silent sleep of exhaustion. The stillness haunted me.

On every previous experience in the Antarctic, when out on the trail, there had always been my dogs to greet me in the morning and raise a happy bedlam of anticipation. But now there was only a great stillness, made all the more absolute by the sound of human breathing in a lone little tent surrounded by hundreds of miles of frozen beauty.

The blue sky was like a painting of the past, a record of something that could not be repeated. Not a breath of air was moving in the lifeless, endless white stretch of frozen space.

I sat on one of the sleds in meditation, my head bowed and my ears reverberating with the roar that such silence produces in the Antarctic. It was hypnotic, and I felt almost in a trance on the border of another world. There is no other place on earth so void of life, so silent, so white, and so deadly.

Far overhead wild-looking clouds lashed the sky, and the quiet about me was like an oasis in a desert of death. At sea we would call it "the devil's smile." But here, on the ice and snow shrouding a lonely land few eyes had ever seen, there was a moment of beauty that made Antarctica seem to me not dead but sleeping.

With a crew of six Seabees under my leadership, we were the Reconnaissance Party of the U.S. Naval Mobile Construction Battalion Special. We had been given one of the most important assignments of Operation Deepfreeze I. It was our job to blaze a 600-mile trail into the frozen wastes of Marie Byrd Land for the tractor train that would follow to construct Byrd Station, when the Antarctic night had come and gone.

The International Geophysical Year was coming up in 1957–58, and the United States Government was co-operating in the unified effort of many countries to record simultaneously all over the world phenomena such as weather, magnetism, gravity, antiglow, and other geophysical elements. The U.S. Navy was engaged in supporting the Antarctic phase of this world-wide program in a great overall expedition called Operation Deepfreeze. The preliminary phase, known as Operation Deepfreeze I, had been designed to establish bases for the use of U.S. scientists.

The plans for the scientists during the International Geophysical Year did not concern me. My job was with the military forces that would support it. I had been assigned to Task Force 43 as a technical advisor and member of the staff. The Task Force included a fleet of seven ships (icebreakers, cargo ships, and tankers) and a Naval Mobile Construction Battalion of Seabees equipped with sno-cats, weasels, and tractors with the support of a Naval Air Squadron equipped with various types of planes as well as helicopters.

The Task Force plans had called for setting up one base at McMurdo Sound in Queen Victoria Land, another in or near the Bay of Whales over four hundred miles to the east, to be called Little America Station, and two smaller stations, one at the South Pole itself, and one to be called Byrd Station at Latitude 80° South, Longitude 120° West in Marie Byrd Land, some six hundred miles east of Little America.

Byrd Station was my "baby" and I had been given a free hand in organizing and planning the laying of the difficult trail that we were blazing and would later use to haul supplies and equipment by tractor train.

After days of search and backtracking and anxious moments, we had marked our way through forbidding crevasse areas pockmarked with millions of dark, ugly-looking holes, found a ramp, and finally gained the plateau. As I looked out into space over the great white ice shelf that had given us so many spine-tingling hours, the spectacle held me spellbound.

From the edge of the plateau I had an unobstructed view of the panorama that unrolled before me. To the west could be seen every rise in the Ross Ice Shelf, the snow hills, the valleys, and the broken confusion of the twisted terrain we had just traveled over.

To the north were the Rockefeller Mountains. They stood

out in lonely splendor, the sharp-pointed peaks, some of them snowcapped, looking like monsters rising out of the Barrier, but beautiful as the sun shed violet rays on their glacial sides and cast dark shadows on the way down. Into this picture, for me, were etched unforgettable details. I had climbed one of those peaks in 1940, and I had been on this plateau when its aspect was not so kindly.

The view to the east and south showed another side of Antarctica. Here there were no colors, nothing pertaining to life or beauty—nothing but a gray void of sky above an endless stretch of white, sandlike snow and ice, a picture of awesome desolation and lonely silence that could give birth, without warning, to an overwhelming howling wind that bit to the bones of men who dared to face it.

We had now marked 250 miles of trail with the International orange flags and I thought it advisable to scout out the area ahead by air, so an Otter support plane took me on a reconnaissance flight. We flew out one hundred miles ahead on our easterly course. The visibility was perfect. As we gained altitude we sighted Mount Grace McKinley, the MacKays, and a range of mountains still further to the east of these. The horizon was alive with peaks silhouetted sharply against the skyline. Those lonely piles of snow and ice and rock were a thrilling sight, one that has a strange fascination for every explorer. Dick Moulton, Leonard Berlin, and I had camped at Mount Grace McKinley in 1940 on our way to the Hal Flood Range where no man had set foot before us. Three of the mountains there bear our names.

All this, I thought, was an Antarctica which the Navy boys back at Little America V did not know. They did not have one printable word to say about her. None of them had been in the Antarctic before, as I had on two previous expeditions. They could not comprehend why I loved her, in spite of the sufferings I had endured at her hands and which they were now enduring. They had never known the grandeur and beauty of Antarctica; they had seen only the desolate Barrier with its deceptive calm and sudden screeching blizzards, and the treacherous bay ice.

They did not know the Antarctica which Admiral Byrd called "an enchanted continent, . . . luring land of everlasting mystery."

2

SUCH was the Antarctica we knew out on the trail in 1956 before the Antarctic night set in. When we returned to Little America Station after this preliminary reconnaissance trip, we had covered a round-trip distance of 920 miles and had been on the trail for twenty-seven days.

During this period morale at the base had taken a drop. Several tractor accidents and plane crashes which had already beset the expedition had struck fear into many of the men, so that their chief thought was of when they could go home again; they were "fed up" with it already. A few left for home when the *Wyandot* pulled out.

A blizzard swept down on us and raged for three days. Pieces of the Barrier started breaking off into Kainan Bay and floating out to sea.

The mighty icebreaker *Glacier* was the last ship to leave us. Out of more than 1,800 men who had invaded this lonely land, seventy-two of us were isolated on the barren ice shelf at Little America V. Over at Hut Point on McMurdo Sound four hundred miles away there were ninety more of our men.

We were obliged to wait until the last of August for the sun to come back again before completing the final six months of the 1956–57 base-laying preparations for the International Geophysical Year. We were the voluntary American "outcasts" of Operation Deepfreeze I who were to endure the long Antarctic night—a handful of men in the icy front trenches of a scientific assault against the glacial ramparts of Antarctica.

As we watched the *Glacier* disappear in sea smoke, and as the sun sank farther and farther below the horizon and the intense cold began to grip the icy continent, we needed to remember the importance of our mission. The base was not yet fully established or in complete readiness for the long months of darkness. The buildings covered about five acres, and we were surrounded by several hundred acres of caches containing equipment, materials, and provisions lying outside, unprotected. It was vital to get as much of this as possible under cover, and day after day we worked feverishly, fighting the wind and cold.

The job was made even more difficult by the blizzards, which had covered everything with many feet of snow. This meant that the boxes and crates, some weighing as much as four hundred pounds, had to be found as well as excavated, no easy task for men whose hands were freezing and whose eyes were blinded with blowing snow.

The tractors and plows were kept running day and night. With my memories of shoveling out tunnels by hand as we did on earlier expeditions, I was very grateful for these machines from which the snow fell away like paper being scooped up by the wind. But even so it was a thankless job, for every time the track around the base was level and smooth at last, a wind would blow down during the night with drifting snow, and the next day it would have to be done all over again.

The intense cold sapped human strength, cutting down man-hours and working power. The men swore as the wind penetrated their caps, freezing their ears and faces. It is a mistake to think that man becomes used to the cold. He never does. Experience teaches him how to dress and wear his clothes to keep as warm as possible, but the cold South has its own rules, and it is wise not to disobey them. The sense of emptiness was appalling in a world not only void of life in itself, but surrounded by an outer space of darkness that spelled death.

Everywhere we looked, all was the same. There was a tight grip around us and over us, like the clutch of a giant hand that had opened to admit us, and then closed . . . not in a crushing grasp, but slowly squeezing us to death. The vast desolation all around us bore down to meet the feeling of isolation within, the one causing pain and the other a sense of depression verging on panic. Every nerve in one's body seemed to cry out for some way of escape from these surroundings.

I had had this feeling many times when wintering over on my two earlier trips, through eight months of the Antarctic Night's deep freezing darkness and howling blizzards on the Barrier. One never does get used to it. So I knew how the other men, whose first experience it was, felt. But this was not Antarctica; it was but the Barrier that kept men from really knowing her and penetrating her secrets.

We could not see through the dark mist that slowly curled over the Ross Sea and the groaning, heaving turmoil of ice. The icy calm penetrated the very vitals of the human body. Men stopped dead in their tracks as if brought up against a stone wall, and stood silent, looking, expecting . . . trying to see into the dim, cold night. But there was nothing to see.

Suddenly an invisible force would stir the noiseless atmosphere into a fury. The wind howled and screamed as if in outrage at the mournful tune man made it play on the antenna atop the roof of his puny hut. Then just as suddenly it would drop off into a dead calm again.

The milky refraction of the day's last dim light blinds the eyes as it filters through the gathering darkness. The ridges of snow all look alike. Objects stand out like black monsters. A tractor, or a box not yet covered with drifting snow, looms out like a thing moving toward you. Not able to identify it, a feeling of dread sweeps over you and you suddenly shiver with fright, looking right and left for a way to escape. A momentary and senseless panic adds speed to your feet. You run for dear life, not looking back in fear of seeing the Thing that is following. You stumble and fall in the snow as if someone had tripped you. You take a deep breath unexpectedly and draw snow into your lungs, almost gagging.

Oh, yes, it is like this. It has happened to me, and I have seen it happen to others. You scramble up and slip again, your mind almost a blank. Then reason comes to the rescue and slowly the feeling of dread leaves you. The spell is broken and you get up, hurrying into camp where you grin at the sight of friendly faces, and secretly call yourself an imaginative fool. But the terror was very real, while it lasted.

Inside our little settlement under the drifting snow it was a different world of warmth and rest or recreation. There were eighteen buildings, nine on each side of the tunnel that we called Main Street. These were flat-roofed affairs with a door at each end, one leading directly outdoors and the other into the 1,000-foot thoroughfare which enabled the men to reach every other building without exposure. There were movies, radio, hi-fi phonographs, a fine library, and plenty of good food. Everything possible had been provided for our physical comfort and mental diversion through the long Antarctic night at Little America V; and yet, as darkness crept over the great isolated block of ice and snow, there was an undercurrent of dread because no man could escape from it; no eyes could see through it;

and no ships or even planes could get through it until the sun came back again. I was accustomed to all this, but the rest had no real idea of what lay in store for them. With the setting of the sun, it was just now dawning on them how helpless we were.

Some of the men cursed the day they had asked for special duty and volunteered to sail south on Operation Deepfreeze I. All the money in the world could not induce them to come again, they swore. Caught between the awful void outside and being cooped up inside, they wanted no part of it, ever again.

They could not understand my love of Antarctica. Any man, they said, who came down here for the third time, as I had, was simply "nuts." Why *had* I come back to this desolate place? What could possibly induce a man deliberately to submit himself to the ordeal which completely engulfs him if he dares to challenge the spirit of the Antarctic Night? The answer is not a simple one, yet I determined to tell, to the best of my ability, the story of my long love affair with Antarctica. During my third, and I think my last, long Antarctic night, I would tell the tale that has never been told before.

Scientists are drawn to Antarctica by a desire to solve its scientific mysteries; I am not a scientist.

Governments are lured into financing multimillion-dollar operations by the hope of valuable scientific information, the discovery of natural resources, the possible acquisition of territory having practical or strategic value; I am laboring for the objectives of the United States Government in Antarctica, but I am not personally concerned with them.

Several of the Navy boys, when I asked them why they had volunteered for special duty in the Antarctic, confessed that one of their reasons for coming was to save a little money. They knew they could not spend any down in Antarctica; there was nothing to spend it on save the bare necessities that they bought from the ship's store. I am sure that the lure of adventure played some part in the decision of most of these men, but they were not explorers by nature; it was not in them as it had been in virtually all the members of earlier expeditions. We had volunteered for service without pay in the sheer quest for adventure and exploration. The Navy boys could understand that; they were, many of them, quite willing to try anything once—their presence on the great ice Barrier of Antarctica proved it. But having seen what it was like, to ask for it again, and yet again? Ah . . . they had a word for it.

Explorers have been lured to Antarctica for more than a century by the instinctive urge for discovery. Man will never stop until he has sought and found and probed all the unknown places and secrets of nature. It is the lot of some of us to carry on the traditions of man's heritage from pioneering ancestors— to blaze new trails away from civilization.

This is not a heritage that comes to all men, but only to those who answer the call when the opportunity arises, or to those who have the spirit to create their own opportunity. There is ever the urge in such men to set foot where other men have never trod. But I had done all this in my younger years; it was not what brought me back to this icy continent to add more gray hairs to my head at the age of fifty-two. I was here for a third time because it was the climax of a lifelong bewitchment, and the story of that bewitchment is the central thread of my whole life. The spellbinding memories of Antarctica in all her moods conditioned my pulse-beat. I could not have done differently. I had to come back.

part II

THE GREAT ADVENTURE

Byrd Expedition / 1928–30

1

I first fell under the spell of Antarctica when I was a boy of ten in the north of Newfoundland where I was born and where I read by candlelight all I could lay my hands on about the mysterious southern continent.

The wind howled outside, piling up the snow about us and heaving the ice of our rocky Newfoundland coast into a diorama in which I saw the great pressure fringes of the ice-locked land of mystery about which I read and dreamed, and with which I now felt familiar.

Then when the rising sun broke through to reveal the frozen bay and the sparkling shores of Bursey Cove, I would harness up nine of my equally excited dogs to a *komatik,* or Eskimo sled, and go out to practice hunting and skinning seals and to expose myself to the cold. I wanted to be fit and able, when I grew older, to brave the blizzards in which men had perished before me, and to boldly woo the remote and enchanting Antarctica.

I knew from what I read that the very existence of Antarctica had been problematical in the days of my grandfathers; yet it had occupied the maps and the minds of men as a myth for three thousand years or more.

According to scholars of the ancient world, there existed at one time a lovely and alluring land of tropical climate, inhabited by people with a highly advanced civilization. But it seemed to have disappeared from the face of the earth.

If this were true, as many supposed, what became of this land? Some thought it sank beneath the sea. But according to Claudius Ptolemy, the renowned Greek physicist, astronomer, and geographer of the second century, such a lovely land did still exist at the southernmost end of the earth. Ancient maps delineated such a continent as *Terra Australis,* to which were added the words *Nondum Cognito,* because no one of the civilized world of recorded history had ever seen it.

The belief continued until the sixteenth century, in spite of many voyages of discovery which encountered only icy oceans where the maps indicated the outlines of the supposed continent.

Several expeditions were sent in search of it, until finally the voyages of the great navigator Captain James Cook proved that Terra Australis had no existence in the form of its assumed character and contour. And yet, a mighty continent of nearly 6,000,000 square miles, almost twice the size of the United States, was there all the time, and we now know that its climate was once tropical.

What great catastrophe befell, that it should now be embalmed in fifty thousand years or more of ice? Did the earth tilt on its axis, and did this loftiest of continents then slowly glaciate into what is now known as Antarctica? Or did some gigantic convulsion of nature tear the land masses apart, shifting their positions, so that a once tropical land became a land of ice and snow?

We know today that Captain Cook greatly underestimated the potentialities of such a continent. If any land at all lay within the Antarctic Circle, which he doubted, it was by his estimate a country "condemned to everlasting rigidity by Nature, for whose wild and desolate aspect I find no words . . ." and also, "should anyone possess the resolution and the fortitude to elucidate this point by pushing yet further south than I have done, I shall not envy him the fame of his discovery, but I make bold to declare that the world will derive no benefit from it."

Yet today it is estimated by one of our leading scientists, Dr. Harry Wexler, that information yielded by previous smaller explorations of Antarctica has been worth ten billion dollars to radio communication alone. And the meteorological and geophysical research now being pursued by the world's top scientists through the aid of Operation Deepfreeze and the multimillion-dollar projects of other nations in Antarctica is expected to be worth billions to agriculture and other human endeavors—essential even to the future survival of mankind through a better knowledge of the structure of the world and of the atmosphere above it, on which our lives depend.

However, Captain Cook's pessimistic pronouncement discouraged further exploration of Antarctica until the nineteenth century, when the existence of a southern continent or continents was definitely established. Sir James Clark Ross got through the formidable ice pack which had stopped previous explorers, discovered what is now known as the Ross Sea, and sighted the great ice barrier which also bears his name.

Of course, all these future developments and values were unknown to me as a lad in the north of Newfoundland. I only knew that the "myth" had been proved a reality. Men had seen the shores of a mysterious, unknown land at the bottom of the world seventy years before the date of my birth.

This first great period of South Polar discovery came to an end with the return of Ross from his third Antarctic voyage in 1843. At the turn of the twentieth century, so very little still was known about Antarctica that we find historian Dr. Karl Fricker summarizing: "For the geographer, the south polar regions are little more than an emphatic point of interrogation, a frank confession that on every branch of geographic knowledge we stand before a riddle, the solution of which belongs to the future."

However, the most intensive period of Antarctic exploration was to begin. During my childhood, in the seven years before the first World War, Great Britain sent out three expeditions; and Australia, France, Germany, Norway, and Japan each sent out one. Shackleton was in charge of two of the British expeditions, and Scott's last expedition was also in this period. Amundsen planted the flag of Norway at the Pole before Scott got there, and the death of Scott and his companions climaxed the "Heroic Era" of Antarctic exploration.

It was out of the records of these heroic men that I wove my dreams of "the Great White South"; and my dogs were always an essential part of this dream. I knew how Scott and his men had died on the icy Barrier of Antarctica pulling sledges themselves, on foot, with no dogs to aid them. I could hardly wait to grow big enough to follow in the footsteps of these South Polar explorers and prove, as the great Norwegian explorer Amundsen had done, that the dogs I loved and trained and championed were man's best friends and allies in his battle with snow and ice.

We could not have lived without our dogs in the utter isolation of our Newfoundland homeland where we children grew up without ever having seen a tractor or a horse, a train or an automobile. There were not even any telephones in our little village of St. Lunaire, which numbered less than sixty inhabitants.

In the summers I was raised as a cod-fisher on the bleak, rugged shores of the northeast coast of Newfoundland. I was trained to know the sea, and learned how to take care of myself in rough weather or smooth. When the ice broke up we coasted along the shores in our schooner, and as a boy I helped my Dad bring her into a snug harbor on many a stormy night. In the winter I drove the team of dogs, our only transportation. I was hardened by the cold and the blizzards that blew over the coast. I didn't know what the future held, but my dream—of following in the footsteps of the polar explorers whose adventures I lived over and over again—continually beckoned.

Beyond this I knew very little. I learned my three R's in the little schoolhouse on the hill overlooking the sea, and that was all. But we were a happy, God-fearing people, accustomed to privation but rich in human loyalty and family love.

Our days, our nights, our thoughts were those of simple folk. We got up and built our fires with the dry wood split into kindling the evening before. We made our breakfast of rolled oats, toast made on top of the stove, caplins or salt fish roasted in the oven, and a good strong cup of tea. We had our own chickens, grew our own vegetables in the summer, and picked fresh berries on the rocky hills.

Our daily work started in the stable feeding the cattle. Most of us kept a few sheep, with both cows and goats for milk, and pigs for salt pork. Then the dogs were harnessed; wood hauled, sawed and split; our dogs fed their one daily meal of fish or seal meat; and the rest of the day was spent knitting twine for our fish traps to be used the next summer when the fishing season opened.

Everyone accepted this life, asking nothing more. I accepted it, too, but I did ask something more. I looked out over the ocean and saw other lands beyond. I looked to the north and in my

mind's eye saw Iceland, Greenland, Baffin Bay, and the North
Polar Sea. But mostly I looked to the south, and there I saw
not the great continents and tropical lands of which my teacher
and elders spoke, but the great ice ramparts of Antarctica. They
stood there silent, challenging, forbidding, against a background
of mountains rising from a frozen continent upon which the
stars shone for half the year, and the sun for the other half.

Why this intrigued me so, I did not know; but it made me
restless. When I was out hunting seals, or sailing over the ice on
a *komatik* behind my team of dogs, I felt that I was getting somewhere. I felt that I had to go on beyond the life I was living;
I had to work harder, to toughen myself, to learn more.

Sunday was a day of rest; we did no work, for we kept the
Sabbath holy . . . but my thoughts were always thousands of
miles away.

Once in a while, when our young minister was in another
parish, the good medical missionary from St. Anthony visited
us and preached the sermon. Then I sat up and took notice.
For this was Sir Wilfred Thomason Grenfell, the medical missionary and author who was superintendent of the Labrador
branch of the Royal National Mission to Deep Sea Fishermen.

Dr. Grenfell was an old friend of my family. All the fisher-
folk of the northern coast of Newfoundland and Labrador loved
the good doctor who had cared for them so many years. The
old folks all remembered and used to tell how he had come from
England as a medical missionary to care for the fishermen and
their families when there was not a doctor on the coast. It was a
time when he was badly needed, for many of the people were in
great distress and dying of tuberculosis. Others had beriberi,
and almost all had bad teeth. Many suffered from accidents,
slashes and broken limbs that they could not themselves properly
set or care for. Many times this good doctor had stayed in our

home when he made the rounds to visit the sick and preached in our little church. He had known me since I was a baby; and I was always thrilled in his presence, for somehow he seemed to me to represent a bridge to what was beyond the horizon of our little world in St. Lunaire.

When, one day, he invited me to visit him sometime, it became a secret objective. When I got a little older, and could travel further alone, I planned to do so. Dr. Grenfell was my gateway to another world.

2

ONE winter day I hitched up my dogs and set out for St. Anthony. A blizzard blew down and we were caught in it; but the dogs kept on going, and I did not turn them back. On through the blinding snow and into the dark of night they followed the trail to St. Anthony and Dr. Grenfell's Mission Hospital.

The doctor was distressed and amazed when he opened the door and I stumbled in out of the blizzard, so far from home alone.

"What's wrong, Jack?" he asked me anxiously. "Are any of the folks sick?"

I shook my head.

"Then why are you out in weather like this?"

His anxiety made me afraid to tell him. Had he forgotten that he had invited me?

I said, "May I have something for my dogs to eat?"

"Of course. Of course." He smiled then. "And for you, too, Jack. Then we will talk. But it seems to me you put a very great and unnecessary responsibility on God to start out on such a journey at this time of year alone."

"I was not alone, Dr. Grenfell. I had my dogs."

"Yes," he said. "You had your dogs. I know."

We understood one another then.

When the dogs were cared for, Dr. Grenfell prepared warm food for me and said, "Now tell me, Jack, why did you come?"

I said, "I want an education."

He didn't laugh, but a little smile twitched the corners of his mouth.

"So that is what it is," he said. "You come all this way through a blizzard because you want an education. Very well, then. You shall have one, Jack. If you are willing to work for it when you get there, I can send you to the United States for that purpose."

So that was how I came to follow the relentless urge within me which forced me to leave the safe haven of my boyhood in search of greater knowledge and far places.

It was not enjoyment that drew me on, for I was often miserable. When I came to the United States and walked the streets of Boston in an overcoat twice my size, I was lonely and bewildered by the crowds of people, the streetcars, and the thousands of automobiles. I felt people were staring at me and I was terribly homesick.

I attended Wentworth Institute in Boston, studying to be a machinist, worked summers on a private yacht, and took International Correspondence School courses at night. I left Wentworth to spend a year at the Missionary Institute in Nyack, New York.

Then one day in 1927 I picked up a newspaper and read an item that electrified me. Commander Byrd of the U.S. Navy was planning to lead an expedition to the Antarctic. I had read all about Commander Byrd's flight over the North Pole, and I would have given all I had to go anywhere with such a man. Now he was going to the one place in all the world that I had most dreamed about since boyhood.

One sentence of the news item set me afire with hope and anticipation: *He is taking with him ski men and dog drivers.*

I sat down at once and wrote the Commander a letter offering my services.

After many anxious days of waiting I received a notice that Commander Byrd was not selecting his men until early spring, but that my name would be considered.

I did not then realize that I was but one of 50,000 applicants, and that the name of an unknown youth would receive scant attention. It did not enter my head that after all my years of dreaming, those dreams might not come true. All that was needed was the opportunity. The opportunity was at hand. I was going, of course. So I went to New York in order to be nearer when word came to report for duty, getting a job with the Hudson River Day Line while waiting.

Spring came and passed into summer. I heard nothing. My name was not among the few who had been selected from the many applicants.

I concealed my disappointment and asked my employer, Mr. Horner, to write me a letter of recommendation. He knew what I was waiting for, and wrote me a wonderful letter of recommendation addressed to Commander Byrd.

On my first day off from work, I got up early to go down to Todd's Dry Dock to look over the ship which was going to the South Pole. I had been watching for this chance ever since I had read that Commander Byrd was purchasing the *Samson,* and that she was coming over from Norway.

The *Samson* was an old ship, but I knew that she was a stout one. She had been built in Norway more than fifty years before, for the sealing trade, and I had heard of her even in Newfoundland. At one time Amundsen had been a member of her crew. She was built to smash ice and stand the pressure, but she had a mighty trim-looking figure, almost like a schooner with her three masts. The cross-yards, however, showed that she was a barque, square-rigged on the foremast and mainmast, which meant that we would have to go aloft to set sail. Only the mizzenmast was fore-and-aft rigged like a schooner so we could raise sail from the deck. She was 185 feet long; 31 feet wide; something over 500 tons; double decked, with a quarter-deck; and she had an auxiliary engine. Commander Byrd had her in dry dock to fix her over. He had renamed her *City of New York*.

One look was enough. I was determined to go on her. I would ship as a seaman, if they would have me. If not, then I would be a stowaway. Such was my youthful determination.

I asked the gateman at the dock when she was sailing.

"Oh, in a week or two, I guess."

"Where is the Captain?"

"He's not here. That wouldn't do you any good, anyway. You'd have to see Commander Byrd."

"Well, where is the Commander, then?"

"His headquarters are over at the Biltmore Hotel."

So I went to the Biltmore and found the expedition office on the fifth floor. Commander Byrd wasn't there. But I saw a man named Charlie Lofgren who asked me what I wanted. He had a strong face and keen eyes. When he looked at me I liked him, and began to feel better. I told him my story, and gave him Mr. Horner's letter of recommendation.

There was a flash in Charlie Lofgren's eyes as he looked up from the letter.

"Bursey," he said, "where have you been all this time? We are leaving in a couple of weeks or less."

"I have been trying to figure some way of getting on the expedition. I never heard from my application."

"I'm afraid you are too late now," Charlie said. "We have

our men all signed up, but I'll do my best for you. Let me have this letter, and I'll show it to Commander Byrd. Come back tomorrow."

The next day Charlie said, "I'm sorry. I haven't had a chance to take your letter up with Commander Byrd yet. But I'll do my best, because I believe you to be a damn good man."

That "damn" made me feel better, because the uncertain waiting was getting me down.

Next morning I was at the Biltmore again, before the expedition office was open. Charlie Lofgren grinned when he came in and saw me.

He said, "Bursey, if you can come back here at eleven o'clock, you will have a chance to see Commander Byrd for yourself."

I was back long before eleven, and I waited until one o'clock before it was possible to see the Commander.

Then suddenly all the tension and anxiety left me. I was unprepared to find a man who was so quiet, efficient, unassuming, and easy to meet.

I thought: There is something in his eyes that is still like a boy. I'll bet he loves dogs, and will understand why I am here.

When Charlie Lofgren introduced us and we shook hands, I thought: This man is all that stands between me and the Antarctic.

The only remaining obstacle was before me, but I was not made to feel that it was formidable. It did not occur to me that if his list was filled up and so limited, he could not take me on and leave someone else off unless there was a voluntary vacancy. But it did occur to me that if this man should say, "No," that would be the end of the matter. The boyish impulse to ship as a stowaway vanished in the presence of a simple honesty that I could never betray.

When the Commander looked up from reading my letter of recommendation, his eyes were thoughtful as he said, "So you come from Newfoundland."

"Yes, sir."

"And you are a dog driver?"

"Yes, sir."

There was a little smile as he asked, "Have you got adventure in you?"

"Yes, sir. I am full of it!"

"I suppose you can skin a seal."

"Yes, I can do that, too." Then for good measure I added, "And I know ice and snow. I know sailing ships and the sea."

The Commander smiled, but then his face became serious.

He said, "I can promise you nothing. All our men are signed up. We have had to turn down nearly fifty thousand applicants. All I can say is that I will see what I can do. I will let you know."

But the week passed and I heard nothing.

One morning on my way to work a girl stopped me and said, "Mr. Bursey, what is this I hear about you?"

I recognized her then as one of the telephone operators at the Hudson Day Line office. "What have I done now?" I asked her.

"Why, a man called up last night after you left and said you were to report at the Byrd Antarctic Expedition Headquarters immediately. And I heard Mr. Horner saying that you would have to leave us, because you were going to the South Pole!"

At Expedition Headquarters, instructions were waiting for me to report to Captain Melville on the *City of New York* immediately. I was on my way at last.

On the 25th of August, when we sailed, the weather was dismal. I remember it now, but at the time it made no difference at all to me. The dock and decks were a madhouse as we worked up to the last moment squaring everything away on the over-loaded little ship amid a bustle of friends and relatives of members of the expedition, some of whom were staying aboard to return with the pilot ship or the tug from out in the harbor.

There was no one I knew, and if I had been less excited I would have felt lonely. I was the only one, I think, except for my Norwegian shipmates, who had no one in the States to see him off. That is why I was surprised when a young chap whom I had never seen before came up to me. He told me he was Doug Burke, from Newfoundland, and when he had heard I was the only Newfoundlander on the expedition, he wanted to wish me good luck and *bon voyage.*

Oh, that was a great day for me when we pulled away from the pier and I was at the wheel where Amundsen had once served his turn to northward, heading out at last for the Great Unknown. Commander Byrd, who would join us later in New Zealand, and his wife and son stayed aboard until we reached the pilot ship. Mrs. Byrd told us all she would keep in touch with our mothers and wives, and when she shook my hand, she said she would send my mother the *New York Times,* with all the stories of the expedition. Russell Owen, a *Times* correspondent, was going along with us, so for the first time in history the public would be provided with a running account of an eyewitness to an Antarctic expedition.

Before we had gone very far out of the harbor, two stowaways were discovered and sent back with the tug. I felt sorry for them and felt a great sense of gratitude at my own good fortune. Later a third stowaway was found, but it was too late to send him back until we reached Panama, our first port of call.

The last ship to salute us on our way out gave three sharp blasts of her whistle. The sight of the giant *Leviathan,* wishing *bon voyage* to our little vessel, sent a pulse of pride through my veins and brought tears to my eyes. I was off on my first Antarctic adventure, the fulfillment and climax of the dream of my boyhood.

Ninety-one days after leaving New York, we reached Port Chalmers, New Zealand. A tug took us in through the Narrows, and after being cleared by the doctor and the customs officials, we pulled into the dry dock for repairs.

When we went ashore, I went off by myself to visit the monument built in memory of Captain Scott and his death in the Antarctic. This was the man whose life had been woven into my boyhood dreams of the Great White South. It saddened me to think of what he had suffered, and how nobly he and his men had faced death—a death that seemed to me so unnecessary, and thus more tragic.

People say of such things, "God's will be done," but I cannot believe God wills human tragedies that might easily have been prevented. The faithful huskies had saved the lives of Eskimos for generations before the rest of the world knew they existed. They had saved the lives of many a white man since, including my own; I would not have dreamed of tackling snow and ice without them. I felt sure that God was with those unfortunate men painfully trudging their last steps on the great ice fields of Antarctica; but the dogs that He created to be man's best friends and allies under such conditions were not with them. I regarded these men as martyrs to this lesson.

3

WHEN the *City of New York* came off the dry dock, we took
her up to the pier in Dunedin alongside our supply ship, the
Eleanor Bolling, and started unloading and reloading at the
same time.

Norman Vaughn, Fred Crockett, Ed Goodale, Arthur Walden, and I went down to Quarantine Island to bring the dogs on
board. They had come out on the whaler *Sir James Clark Ross*
under the supervision of Walden, a Yukon veteran from Alaska.
Amid the deafening tumult of eighty-five dogs all howling at the
same time, we put their crates on two barges and were towed to
the ship by a tug. There was hardly enough space on the ship
for them all. Our little barque was so heavily loaded that I'm
sure all the people who came to the pier to see us off thought she
would never reach the Bay of Whales 2,400 miles away on the
northern barrier of Antarctica. Her bunkers were full of coal, and
between the decks were stacked provisions. Furs filled the cabin,
bunks and clothes bags the forecastle, and there was just enough
room to squeeze near the mess table. On deck we had two portable houses, the radio towers, the Fairchild plane, aviation gas,
oil, and more coal. Besides all that, we had the dog equipment,
sleds, skis, and snowshoes, as well as all the dog crates, eighty-five

howling dogs, and fifty-four men. There was not a clear space on deck big enough to put your foot, and in order to go from forward to aft, you had to walk along the rail and hold fast to a life-line.

The tug *Dunedin* towed us out through the Narrows while the *Eleanor Bolling* followed behind. Many small boats cruised around us, part of a big send-off given by the friendly New Zealand people, all seemingly tremendously interested in our expedition. At the Narrows the *Eleanor Bolling* took us in tow, in order to save our coal. All sails were set and we were on our way, making pretty good speed.

The very first thing I did was to take stock of the dogs. Arthur Walden had with him his own team of Chinook huskies which he had bred on his farm in New Hampshire. His leader, Chinook, was already famous for his keen intelligence, and he was undoubtedly the best dog of the lot. There were many fine dogs, but even the best of them were in pretty bad shape after the long trip at sea. I soon discovered, however, that I had little choice. The other dog drivers had come down from New York with the dogs, and en route had picked those they thought were the very best. Each of them had already chosen nine dogs for his team, and I was told that I could choose my team from the balance of the lot, and that I was also to take care of them for the rest of the trip.

I took one look at my pack of bedraggled huskies and turned away, heartsick with disappointment. What a scrubby, sorry-looking lot! They were so inferior to the dogs I had known in Newfoundland and Labrador, and to the other dogs already claimed, that I was thoroughly ashamed of them. I felt cheated and abused, and thought I had not been treated fairly.

I walked away with anger rising in me, but their whining made me turn back, pity washing out the anger. I noticed how thin and sick most of them looked, how helpless they were in their crates, and how badly they were in need of someone's kind care. The hot trip, the change of diet, the weather, and the rolling of the ship had taken their toll. If ever dogs needed man for a friend, these masterless dogs did. I adopted the whole pack then and there, as they looked at me, expectant, pitiable, questioning. I went to each dog separately, talking to him, assuring him, making friends with him.

Soon I was chuckling to myself, because most of these "left-over" dogs were young, and a dog man never despairs when his huskies are young and there is a chance to put health and strength into their bodies and, through training, intelligence into their brains. I would lavish the best of food and care upon them, and when I reached Antarctica I would hunt for seals, the best possible food for the Eskimo dog. That would soon cure all their ailments.

And then I saw him. He was an older dog, and did not have the small, erect ears of a full-blooded Eskimo. His ears were larger and flapped down disgracefully. There was a touch of mongrel in him; part Chinook, I thought, or perhaps part wolf. But his bones were good, and though they showed through a skinny hide, I saw that he did have the thick coat of hair and plumed tail that meant there was Eskimo in him. He had been brought down from Labrador, just a few miles north of my home in Newfoundland, so he was my neighbor. Born and raised on the same far northern seacoast, we had come thousands of miles to meet each other on our way to the Great White South.

His intelligent eyes had a pleading expectancy in his immediate need and wretchedness. I went up to him and spoke the name of my birthplace.

"St. Lunaire!" I said.

He wagged his plumed tail and looked up into my eyes and

made little noises in his throat as if he was doing his very best to talk to me, acknowledging the name I had given him and accepting me as his master.

I put my hand through the crate to pat his head, and he licked it and whined joyously.

"You old Luny, you!" I said. "Never mind, old boy, you will soon be feeling better. From now on I am your friend and your name is St. Lunaire, but I will call you Luny for short. Do you think you will make a good lead dog? Well, I will give you a chance to find out."

I think it is important to talk to one's dogs. It is just as important for the man as it is for the dog.

One of the men said, "You talk as if you thought a dog could understand you."

"He does," I said. "Not the words, but he understands what I want him to."

People have the idea that a dog can't talk; but he does, in his own dog fashion. You can never come to depend on each other if you don't understand his every growl and bark, the language of his ears, his eyes, his tail, even the angle of his head and of every muscle in the bearing of his whole body. A dog that is understood will live his whole life for you; and will die for you, knowing that you would not permit it if you could possibly prevent it.

The sea got rougher and the *Eleanor Bolling* ahead of us rocked on the heavy swell, causing our tow line to grind and make a lot of noise as it slacked and tightened with the rise and fall of the ship. The dogs kicked up a terrible howl. You could hardly blame them.

St. Lunaire looked for my coming and quieted down when I was near; but with all the other dogs in separate crates, little could be done to stop their noise.

All that some of the men seemed to hear was a pack of wolves howling; sly, mad creatures to be feared and hated, to be tamed only with the lash of a whip. How little they knew them!

Their howling often kept me awake, too; but to me it was the wail of a breed that had been misjudged, forgotten, and uncared for even when they had served well. Knowing their history, I was conscious of the terrible abuse and punishment they had suffered at the hands of the Eskimos and the Indians, who thought nothing of whipping and starving their dogs. But the heart of the true husky remains undaunted, no matter what the conditions, as long as he is still able to hear and respond to the voice of a master who understands him.

All the dogs howled, but what a difference there was between the cry of one dog and that of another! Some were howling from fright and misery, others howled at the wind, at the sea, or at each other. But now Luny was howling for me. There was no mistaking that fact. No empty, aimless howling came from his throat, not since the hour in which we found each other. His voice was sharpened with meaning. He expected to be heard by his new master, and when I spoke he listened, looking at me with intelligent questioning in his eyes, soon learning to understand my voice and to obey it.

A wind came down from the northeast and black clouds drifted in. As the wind grew to gale force, the sea ran in mountains and the *City of New York* rolled her rails in the water and shipped in the seas. All hands were required on deck to lash everything movable, including the dog crates. Before we got to them, we nearly lost some of the dogs as the sea swept over them, drenching them to a sorry, bedraggled-looking lot.

Then the tow line parted from the *Eleanor Bolling*, three men nearly going with it. The order was given to man the windlass; and because we were running up on the *Eleanor Bolling*, we had to shorten sail though we had already reduced to foresail and lower topsails.

It took ten hours to heave in the cable with the old-fashioned windlass. Commander Byrd worked with us, and everyone was in high spirits, joking or singing, all hands working with that will which always unites men in an emergency.

Meanwhile, ahead of us, the *Eleanor Bolling* rolled so far over in the swells, first to one side and then to the other, that we thought surely she would roll completely over. She always righted herself again, but earned for herself the name "The Evermore Rolling" from her crew. When the sea had calmed down a bit, we managed to get close enough to fasten the cable to her again.

Then came the snow and the icebergs which gave us many anxious moments as we picked our way through them in the snow-filled fog, bound for the whaler *C. A. Larsen,* whose Captain Neilson had agreed to tow us through the ice pack.

After the *Eleanor Bolling* had delivered us to the whaler, she cast off and left for Dunedin. We lay quiet for a time by the ice pack and watched the chasers bringing in whales to their mother ship. There were five of these smaller power-boats in the *Larsen's* fleet of chasers whose function was to chase, harpoon, and bring in all the whales that could be found in the big whaler's vicinity. A few of us visited the whaler with Commander Byrd, as Captain Neilson's guests.

This respite after our stormy passage did not mean our troubles were over, although we started our parade through the ice pack with deceiving ease, seven ships in line.

The ice was very slack and many open leads could be seen. The 17,000-ton whaler made her way easily, towing the *City of New York* with the *Larsen's* five chasers stretched out in our wake. Crab-eating seals basked in the sun on pans of ice, looking up at us lazily and apparently without fear. A few Adélie penguins saw us and ran up, chattering together in amazement, wondering what kind of monsters we could be, but still not fearing us.

At first they tried to keep up with the ship, running alongside on the ice. When they found they couldn't, they tobogganed on their bellies, propelling themselves with their little feet. This failing too, they stopped and stood up like tiny statues until we had passed. Sometimes apprehension would seize them, and off they would run.

Then the ice thickened and slowed our progress. It was a tricky business, being towed by the *Larsen*, because she had to go astern in order to butt the ice. Every time she did this there was great danger of the wire towing cable getting caught around the propeller when it slackened. She would signal us by whistle to reverse, but our engines were not very powerful, and by the time they took hold in reverse, the *Larsen* was going ahead again. Then we would hold our breaths, for when the cable tightened you could hang a hundred men on it; and every jerk made the old barque tremble all over.

A few leads of water could still be seen, but the ice was no longer in pans; it stretched out in large sheets. And soon there was nothing on all sides of us, as far as the eye could see from the crow's-nest, but a great silent frozen ocean, glistening in the sun.

The silent peacefulness was short-lived, however. A gale blew down on us with a snowstorm, making it very difficult to pilot the ship through the ice. Often the *Larsen* had to stop and wait for the snow to lighten in order to pick out the best leads. In the blinding snow it was not only hard to see ahead, but there was danger of losing one of the chasers following in our wake, since the leads closed up so quickly after we had passed through. We dared not leave one of them caught in the pack behind us. Not only their lives but our own depended on it, as we soon found out.

The snow got so thick that we could not see the *Larsen* ahead of us. It was a constant stopping and going. For nineteen hours we were brought to a standstill with danger of freezing in.

We managed to break through a mile of ice, then had to stop again with the wind blowing a gale of blinding snow. The ice pack was two hundred miles wide and we dared not linger in it. When the big whaler could see to go ahead, she bucked and backed and our barque trembled from stem to stern with every lurch of the tow line.

Sometimes the *Larsen* got stuck so fast in the pack that without her chasers we might have been caught for good. Receiving her signal to cut her out, they would run half their length up on the ice to break it away from the sides of their mother ship, charging in again and again like little chicks trying to free a mother hen from the grip of a monster. It was a thrilling sight to see.

The *Larsen* had sprung some of the rivets in her iron plates and was now starting to leak, after plowing through 150 miles of the ice pack. But the weather was moderating, and we saw our first killer whale when it came up to blow near the ship in a lead of water that gave us easier passage. Its presence told us that we were not far from the Ross Sea, so called because its southern boundary is the Ross Ice Shelf, both named after their discoverer, Sir James Clark Ross. He was the first man to penetrate the ice pack which bounds and shelters this body of water from the roaring ocean to the north.

Our battle with the ice continued, and in those days there was often a personal element to it. Once when we were going astern the rudder struck a piece of ice and the wheel went out of the helmsman's hands. As it spun around, one of the spokes struck the Captain on the cheek bone and knocked him unconscious.

Another time I was knocked flat on the deck in the same manner. One of the dogs died—not one of mine—but it was our first canine casualty in the Antarctic and increased my concern for the eighty-four dogs that were left of the original ninety. Five had died on the way down.

It took us seven days of such battling before we broke through the pack into the Ross Sea, and saw its black water stretching out ahead of us like a smooth pond in the midnight sun. The sea birds flew around us, filling the air with their strange calls and plummeting into the water after small fish. A school of thirty whales came up to blow, their warm breath rising like smoke from so many chimneys as they spouted into the cold air. The *Larsen's* chasers rounded up twelve of them. In the *City of New York* we started cleaning floors, making beds, and getting things ready to celebrate Christmas in the Ross Sea.

December 25 dawned like a summer day, the weather so fine and the sea so smooth that we could hardly realize we were in the polar region. The sails were all clewed up because there was no wind, but the engine was throbbing and we were making five knots. Aside from this and the splashing of water from the ship's bow, there was no sound; we had entered a world of complete silence where the appearance of Santa Claus somehow seemed incongruous. But there he was (in the person of Professor "Taffy" Davies) laden with Christmas presents for all of us, after a turkey dinner with plum pudding and rum sauce.

Christmas came in by radio and I was surprised to hear my name three times, one of them a message from my parents in Newfoundland. Captain Melville gave out Christmas mail that had been saved for the occasion. Swere Strom played the piano-accordion; John Bayer made wisecracks, impersonating Mary Pickford and other actresses. Arthur Creagh showed us how to escape from a strait jacket and how to get rid of a pair of handcuffs. Then we all sang our heads off, until silence was called and out of that silence came a voice over the radio from 8,000 miles north: The *New York Times* wishing us all a Merry Christmas and a Happy New Year.

With the long journey behind us and the Unknown just ahead, it was a happy and hilarious Christmas. It was topped off by a voice from the crow's-nest calling, "Barrier on the starboard bow!"

Dishes clattered as we dropped everything and raced for the companionway, crowding up on the forecastle head and climbing aloft into the rigging.

It was still a long way off, but there it was: Scott's Great White South—the only coast line of its kind in the world; the great Ross Ice Barrier I had dreamed about, the mother of all southern icebergs, sheer cliffs of ice from sixty to two hundred feet high, extending as far as the eye could see and for hundreds of miles beyond.

Bernt Balchen, senior pilot in charge of our aviation unit, "Chips" Gould, our carpenter, and I got the small cannon we had on board up on the barrick head. We put a load in it, using paper for a wad; Bernt pulled the trigger, and *wham-sling* she went, our salute to Christmas and Antarctica. It was the supreme moment of our celebration.

At 1:00 A.M. we were running alongside the Barrier in the midnight sunlight, feeling like pigmies as we lined the rails of our little ship looking up at the mighty ramparts of Antarctica, towering a hundred feet and more above us. Woe to the ship that might be too close in under those cliffs when they split asunder in the calving of another monstrous iceberg! The prospect staggered our imaginations.

Here and there along the Barrier the warm breath of a whale spout rose up, visible in the cold air. And over us all there fell the first foreshadowing of that strange spell by which a dead world reduces men to silence. It was so still it seemed as if an overpowering presence was sleeping, and the men spoke only in whispers as if fearful of waking her. I spoke not at all, because there was no speech left in me at this climax to my youthful questing.

4

ALL night we sailed along the Barrier, staying a respectful distance away from the towering and often cavernous ice cliffs that might split and crumble at any moment.

In the morning we sighted the mouth of Discovery Inlet, but it took us another three hours to get there. Here we made the ship fast to the bay ice, which was frozen solid between the perpendicular walls of ice on either side of the inlet. These walls, in some places smooth and in other places hollowed out, ranged up to one hundred feet in height.

We were all glad to stretch our legs and could not resist throwing a few snowballs at each other. Commander Byrd set out at once with a party of ski men to explore the inlet for a possible base site and a landing field for the airplanes. Meanwhile the dogs were let loose on deck, and it was bedlam. They leaped the rails to the ice, rolled and fought and yelped with excitement.

The first thing I did was to look for seals, for dog food. Several of us followed the ice-edge for some distance until we found a few, which we killed. While they were being pelted, we dog men went after our teams to pull the meat to the ship.

We had a great time putting the dogs in harness. They were

so wild that we had all we could do to catch them. A mist began
to spread around us and the sea started rising and falling in
swells that broke up the ice all around the ship. As we hurried
to get the dogs back on board, great cracks appeared which the
dogs were afraid to leap, so we had to pull and carry them.
Killer whales were blowing along by the edge of the heaving ice
as large floes split off and drifted out to sea. Commander Byrd
and his party returned just in time, having failed to find a suitable base site. He gave orders to pull out at once. The ship's
whistle sounded to call in all hands, and we set sail for the Bay
of Whales, seventy-five miles further eastward.

It was after midnight, but daylight was continuous. We had
all sails set, to save using the engines. The only sounds were those
of the wind in the rigging, the ship cutting the waves, and from
time to time a reverberation like distant thunder as the Barrier
calved another iceberg. The tortured cliffs of ice we passed
ranged from 75 to 125 feet in height.

We rounded West Cape at 1:30 A.M. the next night in a
shifting haze of mist. A current was running against us, so we
had to clew up all sails and start the engine in order to tie up
to the bay ice.

When we were near enough to jump, I leaped the rail and
was the first man on the ice in the Bay of Whales. Paul Siple
followed me. Paul was the Boy Scout chosen from six Eagle
Scout contestants in the United States to accompany the expedition. We soon had a hole dug in the ice for the ice anchors;
then the ice started to break off, so we couldn't stay there. We
took in the anchors and steamed over to the east side of the
bay where we tried it again. This time we found solid anchorage,
and proceeded to take possession of the place, not dreaming
that it was inhabited.

But almost immediately we were approached by a welcoming

committee of three Adélie penguins and a few skua gulls. The gulls swooped around overhead, looking down at us. The Adélies very modestly walked up to Paul and me and examined us gravely. Then they looked at the ship and back at us again, seeming to ask us questions that we could not answer to their full satisfaction.

When we started running around with the shovels and anchors they thought we were wild creatures indeed, and that it would be wise to put a little distance between us. They did not panic, but merely walked away about fifty yards and stood looking at us as if they owned the place. And as I watched them, the strange feeling came over me that they did. We were the intruders.

This impression was strengthened by the killer whales, fierce-looking brutes, who came right up to the edge of the ice, thrusting their round snouts out of water and looking us over with their piglike eyes as if wondering when we could come close enough for them to find out if we were good to eat. I resolved to keep myself and my dogs at a safe distance, allowing them undisputed possession of the bay.

While Commander Byrd and his party were off scouting for a base site, which they found ten miles away, I hitched up my dogs to give them a little exercise and to see which would make the best lead dog. That was my major problem in preparation for the gruelling work of hauling six hundred tons of freight from the ship to the base site. Did I have a good team, and did I have a really good leader among them?

I had selected eight dogs besides St. Lunaire, and I named them one by one as I got to know them better. I named "Ross" after the British explorer, Sir James Clark Ross; "Brownie" after Captain Brown of the *Eleanor Bolling;* "Byrd" after Commander Byrd; "Siple" after the Boy Scout, Paul Siple; "Bobby" after Captain Bob Bartlett. But "Big Boy" got his name because he tried to bully the other dogs; and "Hawkeye" because he had funny-looking eyes. That left one of my team without a name until I later called him "Coyote" because he was the smartest dog in Little America, but by no means the most intelligent or reliable. In those respects St. Lunaire was his master.

I decided to give each dog his chance, so one by one I tried them over and over, putting first one in the lead and then another, and then back to the first again like a woman trying on hats. But always I came back to St. Lunaire. He responded instantly to every command I uttered. If uncertain, he looked back at me intently, waiting for me to speak the word. If I spoke crossly, he looked at me silently asking the reason. If I scolded him justly for a misdeed such as chasing an Adélie penguin, he hung his head in shame and begged me to forgive him. Sometimes he didn't understand, but he quickly learned; and the other dogs all followed him in mute recognition of that indefinable quality of self-assurance which marks a good leader.

To say that I was proud of my team and of St. Lunaire as a leader would be an understatement and an incorrect way of putting it. I felt a profound gratitude. Under hazardous conditions where a man must depend on dogs as an essential part of him, like his hands or feet, all he can do is thank God for them if they prove reliable.

This welding of a team of dogs to their leader, and of the leader to his master, is something that requires patience and time. It is not achieved quickly; and because it depends so much on both dogs and master, it is often never achieved at all in its full perfection. In all my life, I never had another team like this one, nor a lead dog like Luny.

St. Lunaire became the prize lead dog on the Barrier,

second only to Arthur Walden's wonderful Chinook. And when Chinook wandered off one day and never came back, there was only St. Lunaire who could qualify to lead with his team all the other teams on the most important, and as it turned out, the most dangerous journey of the expedition.

Meanwhile, as my dogs got tempered into a unit of teamwork, they became the fastest in Antarctica, hauling 1,000-pound loads ten miles to the base, and then racing back for another load; forty miles per day, day after day, unless prevented by blizzards. One day we broke the record with three trips, a total of sixty miles. On other occasions, my team hauled record-breaking loads of as much as 2,500 pounds. Not one dog did I lose through overwork or sickness; and while we had many narrow escapes on the crumbling bay ice, and later in crossing Antarctica's most dangerous crevasse area, together we survived where man or dogs alone would have had small chance of doing so.

There were nine teams in all, and nearly every morning there was a ten-mile race to see who would get to the ship first, for the first load. We were living in a little settlement of tents called "Dog Town," near the site that had been picked for a base at Little America. With Luny leading, I seldom failed to win that race over the bay ice to the ship, and Arthur Walden always came in second. Four of the others, Mike Thorne, Arthur Berlin, Chris Braathen, and Quin Blackburn, had never driven dog teams before, but they did fine work all during this arduous period of hauling.

The ship was tied up to the bay ice to unload for the dog teams. The ice was always breaking up, and after every blizzard the ship had to move to a different position to find solid ice. We had some anxious moments on the long haul over the bay ice, crossing cracks with 1,700 feet of dark water beneath us, climbing over pressure ridges and making our way over the Barrier with seemingly bottomless crevasses on either side.

Out on the bay ice, Weddell seals would raise their lazy heads as we passed them, and then go off to sleep again as unconcerned as if they never saw us. At first the dogs were wild to get at them, and before I could establish an understanding in the matter, they did.

I had no brake on the sled at the time and was wholly unable to hold them. I even broke my ski trying to stop them. But nine husky dogs obeying the call of the wild were too much for one man whose voice of command was drowned in the din they were raising. The dogs dashed in among the seals and jumped on a big Weddell female. She slashed with her teeth and hind flippers, bellowing and doing her best to get away.

Finally I got the dogs away from her and she hurried for her blowhole, not much hurt. It was one of the few times that I ever had to crack the whip at my dogs.

Many times in those early days our loads turned over, which meant unloading and loading up again; but this was not the fault of the dogs. A pressure ridge was enough to tip the sled, and there were many inclines down which the sled would slip beyond the power of the dogs to hold her. Once the whole team disappeared in the water through a crack in the ice which had been snowed over; but as they were all fast to the gang-line in their harnesses I was able to pull them out one by one, though it took me some time to do it. They wagged their tails and licked my hands and face as if in gratitude, then shook themselves, and away we went again.

There were a few days when we couldn't travel because of snowstorms. I woke one morning to hear the tent rattling like a piece of sheet iron; I thought surely the wind would blow it down. A blizzard was raging outside, and hungry as I was, I hated to crawl out of my warm sleeping bag even to eat. We were all pretty tired, and blessed the blizzard when someone came around to each tent advising us to roll over again for another snooze as a radio message had come from the ship: "Hold the dog teams at the base until further orders."

At noon, however, we got another message saying that all the dog teams were to proceed at once to the ship. The wind was howling and whistling around the tent, playing tunes on the guy wires. I had to lean against the wind to hitch up my team. As I talked to each one of my dogs it was plain that they did not like the idea of going out in the blizzard any better than I did. But I persuaded them that this was the sort of thing we would have to get used to in Antarctica, and we were soon on our way to the Bay of Whales.

To enter the bay, we had to cross a big pressure ridge. I gave this very little thought as I drew near to it, because I thought it would be the same as it had been the day before. But pressure ridges are always changing shape and building up, and during the night and morning this one had been disturbed more than usual. Before I realized it, my dogs had jumped a crack in the ice and were floundering around in the water.

Luny was lucky, for he gained a purchase with his forepaws on the edge of the ice and managed to crawl up the other side. But if I had not been quick enough to stop the sled from going in the water on top of the dogs, Luny would surely have been dragged down, too.

With Luny on the ice to lead and pull them, the other dogs soon managed to clamber out after him. Then they pulled the sled so hard that I was able, being on it, to cross over on partially submerged ice by diverting the sled to skirt the edge of the hole through which the dogs had broken. They

were raring to go again because the dunking had chilled them
and they could warm up only by running. So I gave the word,
and a fast run brought us through the pressure area and out
on the open bay ice.

Here, however, the weather was so thick that we could see
very little. We were following the old trail that we had been
using for days and which the dogs knew well, but the ship had
moved because of crumbling ice and though I couldn't see it,
I knew I would have to turn the team to eastward.

We were running before the wind toward the open bay
where the ice was a jumble of broken pieces. We were sailing
right along, the dogs going at top speed; and I mean sailing,
because the dogs were using their tails high up over their backs
as sails. Still unable to see the ship, I figured on driving as
near to the edge of the water as possible and following it eastward until I came to the ship. That way I could not miss her.

So I was listening anxiously for the roar of the water as
the wind rolled it up, but couldn't hear anything above the
tumult of the wind itself, fast driving us toward the open sea.

Whether I could stop the team in time would be the supreme
test between St. Lunaire and me. This was the first real crisis
in our relationship. It would be bad enough to run over the
edge of the ice into the Bay of Whales, but it was better to
discover right here whether or not I could fully depend on St.
Lunaire under such conditions, if we were to work together in
handling our team through the dangerous crevasse area that
I expected to encounter in the trail-blazing advance on the
Queen Maud Range of mountains.

The blizzard blacked everything out beyond a few yards of
visibility. If the dogs did not choose to respond to the command of my voice there would be no way of controlling them
when we reached the open water. I could slow the sled by

braking it, if I could see well enough to know when to do so; or I could roll off the sled and let the dogs run off without me; but there were no reins, as with a horse.

"Take it easy, Luny, old boy," I sang out. "We must be getting close."

St. Lunaire immediately slackened pace to look back at me questioningly, and a grateful thrill ran through me. The rest of the team slowed up to match his pace. I braked the sled, so it would not run up on them.

I said, "Whoa, boy!" and together Luny and I brought the team to a full stop.

"*Yath!*" I called.

This meant to go ahead again, and the whole team responded.

I shouted "Gee!" above the howling of the blizzard, and Luny responded immediately. He turned to the right and the whole team followed him.

My heart slowed down a bit; for there, to the left of us, was the open water. And for the first time, in those moments of apprehension, I felt that my team was truly a part of me. I would not hesitate to trust them anywhere, now.

We were driving across wind and going slower because we were off the trail. But the ship was as yet nowhere in sight.

The sled broke through seal holes and small cracks as the dogs kept going, pulling the runners out of the water. Then the ship came into view, her nose stuck up against the bay ice which was breaking off. Small ice pans slapped and drifted along by her side. From the ship the crew motioned me to stop, for the ice was dangerous around her. St. Lunaire obeyed at once as I gave the command to halt.

A few of the men were trying to get the supplies onto the ice where the dog teams could drive up to load before conditions got any worse. I was forced to wait for my companion team, as Commander Byrd had given orders that two teams were always to travel together, in order to help each other in time of trouble. We had started out at the same time but in ten miles had lost each other in the blizzard. When the other driver arrived, we loaded our sleds and headed up the bay with the wind in our faces. The ice did not look good, but we hoped to shorten the trip by making a "V" toward the old trail where the going would be much better. I was in the lead, but shortly after we left the ship, the other driver veered off and made his own track. He was fifty yards away when my dogs started breaking into a hole. I urged them on and they got across, but the sled with its heavy load started to break through.

The dogs stopped with the sled balancing on the edge of the hole, unable to pull it out. I grabbed the gang-line in one hand and put all my strength and weight on it to prevent the load from going backward down through the ice. With the other I whipped out my knife. If possible I would save the precious load of coal, but if my strength gave out and I could hold the heavy load no longer, I would cut the gang-line and save my dogs from being dragged in after it.

Yelling at my partner, I held up my hand with the knife in it to show him I was in trouble. He looked around at me, but kept on going.

Luny looked at me expectantly, but he and the other dogs were lying flat on the ice, tired out, and I could give them no orders. The sled was so precariously balanced that I did not dare to urge them forward for fear of making the situation worse. Meanwhile, the sled was slowly sinking as the ice gave way beneath it.

On the ship a mile away, the lookout in the crow's-nest saw

me and gave the alarm. Arthur Walden and Arthur Berlin started running toward me. With this hope I hung on, although I felt my arms could hardly endure the strain another moment; when they arrived, I had the knife to the gang-line. With the help of the team, the three of us finally managed to get the sled, with its precious load of coal, out to safety. By now the other driver was far in the distance and Commander Byrd was watching him.

The driver said afterward that he thought I was only joking or just caught in a snowbank. But in any case he had broken the law of the trail in not coming to help me, so his team was taken away from him and given to Paul Siple. Paul had never driven dogs before, but he caught on and quickly became an excellent driver.

So on we went again. It was all in a day's work in Antarctica.

The bay ice got so bad that the ship had to move once more. This time she tied up by the side of the Barrier, which was higher than the ship at this point. The *Eleanor Bolling* arrived from New Zealand with more cargo and our first mail delivery on the Antarctic continent.

The new trail from ship to base was shorter and easier for the dog teams, but there was a price to pay for it. Walden, Siple, and I had just left with our loads when we heard the ships' whistles blowing in sharp alarm. A piece of the Barrier had broken off and tons upon tons of ice fell upon the *Bolling*, turning her partly over.

One man was thrown into the water; another caught a rope as he went over the rail and hung halfway between the water and the top of the Barrier. Both were rescued and there were no fatalities, but it was a sobering experience, and it took plenty of work to get the ice off the *Bolling*.

Her cargo was finally unloaded on the ice, and when I brought our mail down from the base, a rope was put around my waist and Bernt Balchen held fast to the other end in case the Barrier should break again. I walked out to the edge and threw the mail on board as soon as the *Bolling* steamed in close enough to touch the Barrier.

She left for Dunedin without further mishap and we watched her go, knowing it would be the last we would see of her for many months. There would be no more mail for us until after the long Antarctic night was over.

It was necessary to pile the supplies further away from the edge of the Barrier so nothing would be lost should there be another break. It took three dog teams, including my own, to pull the plane, the *Floyd Bennett,* in safely, and four teams to haul her to the base at Little America.

The snowmobile was finally put into action, and we enjoyed watching her throw up the snow behind her as she sped over the ice. As she could relieve us in pulling supplies from the *Bolling* cache to a safer position, I went back to the *City of New York* where more freight was ready for us to haul.

By afternoon another blizzard bore down on us. When we got to the ship for our loads, the ice was again breaking up around her and we had to stop the teams some distance away. The supplies were man-hauled over the slush and broken pans of ice to the waiting dog teams.

The weather was getting thicker and it was impossible to look to windward. Arthur Berlin and I struggled back to the base with another load, but Walden and Crockett, who left after us, lost the trail and had a hard time finding the base. When they didn't show up, a search party was organized to go out and look for them. They finally came in after dropping one of their sleds and two drums of gasoline.

So we slept in for a couple of days, going out only to feed seal meat to our dogs, who were having a good rest curled up in the snow. The *City of New York* was steaming back and forth in the bay to keep off the ice. But so much pack ice drifted into the bay that when the weather moderated she went out to sea and made an attempt to reach Edward VII Land. Commander Byrd had sighted unknown land beyond this point on plane flights. All the land between the Rockefeller Mountains, 125 miles east of Little America, and the 150th meridian was considered to be British territory since it had been discovered by Captain Scott on his voyage in the ship *Discovery*, 1901–03. Commander Byrd wanted to see how far east he could get from the Bay of Whales in the *City of New York*. He hoped to reach the unknown territory beyond Edward VII Land. While the *City* was gone on this mission, I had my first plane flight in Antarctica.

A few of us went up in the Fokker plane with Bernt Balchen as pilot, and that was when I first began to sense the real immensity of this mighty ice-covered continent. Our base was but a tiny dot in a seemingly endless expanse of coastal Barrier ice which was actually part of the sea, not the land. We were camping on the floating frozen edge of the sea, nowhere near the shore line of the buried continent, whose existence was silently attested to by the distant violet peaks of mountain ranges to the west, south, and east.

To the north stretched the waters of the Ross Sea, dotted with icebergs. To the west the broken and irregular Barrier edge extended four hundred miles or more to McMurdo Sound, where Scott and Shackleton had set up their bases, years before. Seventy-five miles west of the Bay of Whales was Discovery Inlet, where we had first landed. Between Discovery Inlet and the Bay of Whales was a smaller cut in the Barrier which Commander Byrd had named Lindbergh Inlet. Just inside West Cape, which bounded the Bay of Whales, were Floyd Bennett Harbor and Chamberlin Harbor. From there, twenty miles directly across the bay, was our base, now known as Little America I. Thirty miles east of this was Kainan Bay, discovered by Lieutenant Choko Chirase of Japan sailing in the *Kainan Maru*. He landed there in 1912 and made a sled journey across the Barrier to Edward VII Land, which Commander Byrd was attempting to reach in the *City of New York*. We could see the little craft from the air, already on her way back, for the impenetrable ice pack had prevented her from gaining her objective. Inland from this point were two ranges of mountain peaks discovered by Commander Byrd by air while we were unloading the ship. The nearest of these, 125 miles east of Little America, he had named the Rockefeller Mountains. Beyond them was Marie Byrd Land, and then another range which he named the Edsel Ford Mountains.

With the clear weather and the sun shining from the north, the coloring of this otherwise drab and desolate Barrier became indescribable. The clouds in the blue sky were rainbow-hued, the sea reflected the sun's golden rays, and the rolling hills and peaks and cliffs of ice took on all the delicate shading of prismatic reflection. But ugly, jagged, tortuous crevasse areas emphasized the impermanence and insecurity of the Barrier.

How little I dreamed then that ten years later I would set forth on skis with two companions and two dog teams to travel 610 miles into this region to survey some of these mountains and to plant the U.S. flag where no man had ever set foot before. And if anyone had predicted that twenty-seven years later I would live for more than a year at Kainan Bay and blaze a tractor trail into the same region, without a dog to aid me, I would not have believed him.

5

WE settled down to hauling what remained of the supplies. The sun went below the horizon for the first time on February 21, a reminder that winter was coming on. The *City of New York* made ready to leave for New Zealand, and we all gathered, forty-two of us, to see her off, including Commander Byrd who had flown over from the base.

Some of the men on the ship were very much disappointed that they could not stay with us. I felt sorry for them, because I knew exactly how I would have felt if I had been forced to go.

The Commander told them how much depended upon them, and that they were just as important as the fellows who were to stay on the ice. This helped, I guess, but it could not change the way I would have felt about it, and as I knew Arthur Berlin did feel. He had done mighty fine work driving his dogs, the first time he had ever done such a thing. I hated to see him go as much as he hated to leave us. He had become very much attached to his team of dogs, as I had to mine; so I knew how he felt about that, too. He stayed on the ice just as long as he could; and then before he had to get aboard the ship he said good-by to each one of his dogs separately. When he came to Lady, his lead dog, tears ran from his eyes because he knew he would never see her again. I laid my hand on the head of St. Lunaire and he rubbed his flappy ear against my thigh just as if he understood and was grateful that it was not happening to us.

When everyone was aboard, the lines were let go. The ship moved slowly out, and all those aboard and we on the ice stood looking at each other across the widening gap of water. We gave three cheers for the departing crew and they answered with three of their own, but somehow it failed to sound cheerful, or to be cheering.

My mood was mixed, because I had caught the feeling of the men about me and yet I could not wholly accept it as mine. After all, this was what I had come for. This was what I had dreamed about, and the dream had come true; and I think that I fully realized it for the first time in that moment as I stood there watching the ship draw away.

Slowly the *City of New York* disappeared in the vaporlike sea smoke that was blowing over the Bay of Whales. First the hull was blacked out, then the masts and cross yards, making her look like some ghost ship of bygone days. At last she was gone, and the only proof she had been there were the marks her sides had made on the ice.

The silence in the midst of utter desolation was suddenly appalling. Many months were ahead of us before we could ever expect to see a ship again. And now that we were left alone, soon to be sealed off from all the world by the freezing ice pack, not all the resources of all the nations could rescue us if anything went wrong.

Every man was deep in his own thoughts. Some had a far-away look in their eyes. Some had a solemn expression of wonder and puzzlement. Some showed a trace of sorrow. Still, I'm sure there was not a man among us who would have changed places with any other human being.

I looked toward my team of dogs, surprised that not a sound came from them. They were looking out to sea, and I wondered if they could possibly realize that they too were stranded here on this ice barrier, most of them never to leave it alive.

Ordinarily the Eskimo dog is never quiet unless he is very tired. He is always growling at the next dog, or trying to pick a fight. But both dogs and men were still, as in a trance. With a last look to the north after the ship which was no longer visible, I started to move my team slowly. Then the stillness was broken by the whine and howl of a husky — a mournful sound, as if he, too, were beginning to feel the loneliness.

After the ship's wake had quieted, the Bay of Whales came to life. In came the killer whale, that scavenger of the south, looking for a seal that might be singled out on a pan of ice drifting with the tide. We could see his dreaded triangular fin.

Both men and dogs began to move, getting ready for the race to Little America. The plane took off and circled the ship after it had been swallowed from our sight by sea smoke; Commander Byrd had chosen to return to the base on my sled with his little fox terrier, Igloo.

Other teams were already on their way, but we had ten miles to show the Commander what my team could do. The dogs were in their glory, and the plumed tail of St. Lunaire had never been higher over his back in sheer joy of his leadership as we passed the other teams, one after another, until we held the undisputed lead. And Igloo growled and barked at every team we passed, as if to say, "Get back there now, and see you stay behind!"

It was 24° below zero, and some of the men froze their faces on the trip in. The ship had left none too soon, for during the night the Bay of Whales froze over.

We settled down to the business of getting ready for winter

in a little world of our own, which was still under construction because the *Bolling* had been unable to get through the ice pack with the last three of our five prefabricated main buildings. "Chips" had to do the best he could with lumber from the airplane crates and any other wood he could lay his hands on.

Our main buildings, the Mess Hall and the Administration Building, were set about 150 yards apart to avoid fire hazards. The foundations were dug deep into the snow, the prefabricated houses were set in these, and a tunnel was dug to connect them. Behind the Mess Hall was the Norwegian House, which we called "The Biltmore" because it was a bunkhouse. About a hundred feet to one side of this was a machine shop and storehouse for the aviation mechanics. On the other side was a non-magnetic house for Taffy Davies, our physicist. Another bunkhouse was being planned, adjoining the machine shop, and a photographic darkroom adjoining the Mess Hall. Hanson was building a radio laboratory in a corner of the Administration Building. Our supply officer, George Black, was digging a huge hole in the snow leading off from the main tunnel for his storehouse. The tunnel itself was lined with boxes of provisions until it was so narrow that only the smallest men could get through it without walking sideways.

We dog drivers were detailed to dig tunnels and to kill enough seals to feed the dogs for the remainder of the winter. I had killed and skinned seals all through my boyhood, and this was nothing new to me. But nothing short of necessity could have induced me to kill three or four hundred harmless Weddell seals in cold blood as we now had to do. It was also my job to find some way of storing the seal meat so we could get at it through the winter. I solved this problem by laying the carcasses in rows near the site of the dog tunnels, with space between the seals to prevent their freezing together.

After several stormy days, we were given orders to get ready for the trail. We were to go about forty miles south and return by March 15, which was the date that Amundsen and others had all agreed was the latest it was safe to be out on the trail in Antarctica. This trip would give us experience and would show us what we would be up against next spring when the long trips were scheduled.

The weather was fair next day, so I harnessed up my dogs to try out my wooden runners, which seemed to run easier in low temperatures than iron ones. Charlie Lofgren and I rode down to the Barrier cache at the bay to get some flag sticks to mark the trail we were to make, and we saw the first star we had seen in the Antarctic sky — a sure sign that the long, dark nights would soon be upon us.

Next day a bad blizzard came down with a thirty-two-mile wind at 10° below zero, so we went on with our planning and preparations. But Siple, Thorne, and Blackburn had started out for the Barrier cache with their teams before the blizzard hit us. Siple and Thorne got back to camp, thinking Blackburn was ahead of them. They had all started out together and were in sight of each other until the dense blizzard made Blackburn invisible.

Blackburn did not turn up, so Commander Byrd, Dr. Gould, and Thorne went out as a search party to look for him. They were gone some time, but no trace could be found. Then several search parties were organized, each to go in a different direction with a team of dogs.

Mike Thorne, Vaughan, de Ganahl, and I went toward the Barrier cache, but a little to the east of it. We had not gone far before the blizzard let up enough for us to see something black in the distance. Thorne and I hurried toward it and saw it was Blackburn's dogs. Blackburn, however, was nowhere to be seen. We found him finally in a hole he had dug in the snow. He was so comfortable in it that he would have been content to say there indefinitely, but we routed him out and took him back to camp with us.

Actually, it was the seventh of March before the weather broke long enough so we could harness up our dogs and be under way. There were six of us in the trail party—a radio man, navigator, and four dog drivers. Except for some trouble getting from the bay ice to the edge of the Barrier, our first day out was a smooth one.

The second day we ran into bad visibility. As we could see only a few yards ahead, we traveled roped together as a safety factor if one of us should slip into a crevasse, and by afternoon laid the first twenty-mile depot. We built a beacon with a marking flag on top and a line of flags running east and west of the trail. In the lobster-pot tent we left food for both men and dogs, clothing, a primus stove, and some fuel.

Early the next morning when we were just about ready to start off, we all felt a peculiar little puff of wind pass by. Within five minutes, the wind was up to twenty-five miles an hour and steadily increasing. We made camp again, huddled in one tent and waited to see what would happen.

In no time at all, a storm was raging with winds sixty miles an hour and stronger. The tent rattled so violently we thought it would blow away. A blizzard is the worst thing you can encounter on the trail, especially so late in the season. We crawled into our sleeping bags, and as we listened to the howling of the wind and the beating of the snow on the canvas, a realization of our isolation oppressed us. Nowhere else in the world is this sense of loneliness so keen as on the Antarctic continent, in a tiny tent away from the base and thousands of miles from home.

By the next afternoon it had started to clear a little. Everything was snowed over, there was no sign of our sleds, and some of the dogs were loose. We all saw our first mirage—flags, some distance away. We broke camp and pushed on to the forty-mile depot, where we repeated the routine of building a beacon and laying a cache. We wanted to go on another twenty miles, but after four miles we ran out of flags and decided to return to base, reaching Little America the same evening—the thirteenth of March. On the fourteenth there was such a blizzard that it was all we could do to get out to feed the dogs. We had returned just in time.

Five days later we were back on the trail, with St. Lunaire leading six other teams, headed for the Rockefeller Mountains. One of our planes had been wrecked there in 120-mile winds, and Commander Byrd, who had gone in with the rescue plane, and two other men were waiting for good weather to be flown out. We did not consider ourselves a rescue party, although we were prepared for that possibility if weather conditions continued bad, or if something should happen to the plane. We were primarily an emergency safeguard. But this was the nineteenth of March. We were trespassing beyond the Antarctic date-line for safety, and our lives depended on our dogs.

By the time we laid the forty-mile depot on March 21, many of the men were frostbitten, one of the other lead dogs had given out and had to be hauled on the sled, and the going was very rough. It was not until the next day that the plane could take off from the base. It passed us overhead on its way to the mountains. We were then sixty-three miles from base. Three teams had already returned to Little America, and we were waiting it out to be sure the plane had picked up the men and was on her way home.

In about an hour the plane circled overhead, which meant that all hands were on board and our mission finished. We broke camp, lightened our loads, and at 3:00 P.M. headed for Little America. The temperature was dropping and we had no desire to linger. With St. Lunaire leading, never pausing or losing the trail of flags, we traveled all night. He needed no instructions. The dogs all knew they were returning to camp and there was no stopping them.

The moon appeared for a short time at midnight, looking like a ball of fire, but aside from that and our first glimpse of the waving, weaving curtains of the aurora australis, there was only the light of the stars to guide us. We reached Little America at 4:00 A.M., breaking the Antarctic record for speed, having covered sixty-three statute miles in thirteen hours. The longest previous non-stop march in Antarctica had been made by Amundsen and his party when they traveled sixty-two miles in one day.

6

T H E dog teams got back—and therefore we did. This was what I had always dreamed of: men and dogs against the ice. How little the other men knew what it meant to me!

There was one who seemed to sense it—Russ Owen, the *New York Times* correspondent, and he was greatly puzzled. I would catch him looking at me, and shaking his head in a funny little way as if I were something entirely beyond his comprehension.

The Pulitzer Prize winning book that grew out of his chronicles is perhaps the first wholly informal account of an Antarctic expedition. And not until I saw the book years later did I understand the little smile and the shake of the head when Russ looked at me.

Russ was an observer and not a participant. He disposed of the heart and soul of Antarctic exploration in a single sentence: "The dog teams got back."

From his viewpoint, and understandably so, the dogs themselves were memorable chiefly for their howling and their stench. In speaking of the dog drivers of the expedition he wrote, "Three of them are New Englanders, from near Boston; one is a hardboiled Irishman, another a lad from the north of Newfoundland who is having the time of his life, but having always lived hard he is indifferent about things which annoy the others."

This was my Great Adventure, and he observed it, but he did not comprehend it. I suffered annoyance, disappointment, and distress, like everyone else, but it was all a part of the Adventure. He was right in concluding that I was having the time of my life. But he did not know that the tragic memories of Scott and his men were my constant companions out on the trail, and that the value I placed on my dogs was because of the price they had paid for lack of them.

The dog teams got back, and the men with them. But the observer knew nothing of the thrills and hazards of the world's worst blizzards, bottomless crevasses, and treacherous icy slopes out on the trail; or of making trail with a heavy load pulled by a team of Eskimo dogs in the dark of night or in the deceiving light of the setting sun.

During that first long Antarctic night I had my dogs to care for, and with so many other activities, I never did feel the loneliness and monotony which seem to bother so many men in Antarctica. Fortunately, too, there were many bright moonlight days when I could get outside, no matter how cold it was. Too, we dog men were busy preparing for our long trips in the spring.

I had not nearly so much time to write in my diary as I had expected. Omitting dates, the highlights of my memories ran like this:

Strom and Braathen killed thirty seals today, which cleaned up our seal killing for the dogs. Roald Amundsen killed his last 6 seals on the same day 18 years ago. The temperature is 30° below zero. . . .

The weather is fine so we are pulling in seals all day. This morning when we went down in dogtown we found Shackleton and Muskey, two of Goodale's dogs, dead. They were killed by other dogs while fighting over a female. . . .

I spent all morning digging my dog crates out of the snow, getting them ready for the winter. This afternoon Paul Siple and I started digging a dog tunnel for our own dogs. The tri-motored *Floyd Bennett* was pulled into its hangar where we can work on it in preparation for the spring flight over the South Pole. It took 60 dogs, half the men, and the snowmobile to get it in. . . .

Easter Sunday, March 31, the first holiday since striking the Bay of Whales. Commander Byrd and I took a walk down to Ver-Sur-Mer Bay and saw a sunset that took our breaths away with colors and rich shadings that I had never seen before. A big poker game is going on to see who is to clean out the Crystal Palace (the toilet). . . .

Weather calm at 50° below zero and work is still going on at the tunnels. While we are working at that, another gang is digging a storehouse. Chips is building it out of lumber from the airplane crates because three of the buildings we were supposed to have were still on the *Bolling* when she failed to get through the ice with her last cargo. We are digging tunnels from one house to the other, 150 yards apart, so we can navigate without going outdoors. But we have no electricity, so we will have to use lanterns or flashlights. . . .

Paul and I completed a dog tunnel after many days of hard work. It is seven feet deep, about fifty yards long, and three feet wide. You can imagine how much snow we had to take out of it. It was too hard to be shoveled, so we had to saw it out in blocks. Then the tunnel was covered with crossboards two feet apart, with a roll of wire over them and a roll of canvas on top of that. When the snow drifted over it, the tunnel was pretty warm. We dug holes in the side of the tunnel for the dog crates and chained the dogs so they would have a little freedom to move around without getting at each other . . .

Paul Siple and I started digging a zoology house for "scientific" purposes such as skinning penguins and making souvenirs. Strom, Balchen, Davies, de Ganahl, and Mike Thorne, with his dogs, went to look for Framheim, Amundsen's winter quarters of 18 years ago when he discovered the South Pole. His base was about four miles from here, but the men came back without having found any sign of it. . . .

We finished the zoology house today. We used the small lifeboat as a roof, which gives the top an odd shape. We cut an entrance through to one of the dog tunnels and then dug a hole opposite the entrance to put our penguins in. Pete Demas made a blubber stove out of a gasoline drum which gave out a wonderful heat. We made a little table in the center for skinning penguins. . . .

This is my night on watch. The watchman's duties begin at 7:00 P.M. and last until he lights the fires in the morning. Every half hour he goes out to record weather data, note auroral displays as to time, colors, strength, direction of wind, and other weather conditions. He must make two visits every night, overland if it is not storming, to the Mess Hall. Between times I sit in the library reading by the light of my lantern. Just after taps tonight Commander Byrd came out of his room and gave me his big sealskin coat to put on, because it was quite cold. There is a saying that "it is the little things that count," and I couldn't help thinking of this in connection with the Commander, who is always ready to lend a helping hand to anyone, always thinking about the comfort and discomfort of the other fellow, and what he can do to help him. . . .

The sun rose this morning like a ball of fire but soon disappeared again. It is the last time we will see it for four months. The temperature is 45° below zero. We started digging a gymnasium. . . .

Today it is 50° below, and while a big poker game was going on in the Mess Hall, a naked man came in from out of doors. It was Dr. Coman, who had come from the Administration Building 150 yards away without a stitch on except a pair of caribou socks. A scientific experiment, I presume. . . .

The long night is on, but today there was a beautiful moon with a halo. I took my dogs out for a little exercise, and Commander Byrd rode down the bay with me. Igloo ran alongside the sled, dashing out now and then to race along with St. Lunaire, holding onto the harness with his teeth. . . .

At 4:00 P.M.—11:00 P.M. in New York—we gathered around the shortwave radio to receive messages. There were two for me, but static drowned out everything but my name. The radio is our only connection with civilization and is the most important thing on the expedition. No party is to leave Little America either by dog team or airplane without one; it relieves the leader of a great deal of worrying. What a difference between our modern equipment and what Captain Scott had!

Our gymnasium is the coldest one in the world. It is built of snow, except the roof which is covered with a large piece of canvas over a bamboo framing. When we box or exercise, a gasoline lamp is hung up in the corner where it casts a light over everything. . . .

It is a rule at Little America to have all lights out at 10:00 P.M. After the lights were put out tonight, I decided to go and see Professor Davies (whom we call Taffy) in the photo laboratory, as he was night watchman. When I opened the door I noticed a rather stuffy smell, but thought nothing of it until I walked over to the box where Captain Mac kept his pup, Ski, trying to break him in as a house dog. The pup was almost dead. I could not think what was wrong, because I had been playing with him a little while before. Then I saw that Taffy was acting strangely. Dr. Coman came in and I said, "There is something wrong with Taffy. Better get him out of here." We found the trouble was carbon monoxide gas coming from the gas stove. Both Taffy and the pup recovered after a half an hour of fresh air. . . .

I am trying to write in my diary, but it is quite distracting. At the table, Dean Smith is also writing in his diary and reading some of the funny parts aloud to Russ Owens. George Tennant and Arnold Clark are busy with the cooking. Harold June is sitting on a bench with a bucket full of soapsuds, washing a shirt for himself because every one he has is dirty. With the beard he has, he looks like Santa Claus. There is another gang around the table playing poker for cigarettes. Henry Harrison and Joe Rucker are good at this. They live in the Administration Building and they come over to the Mess Hall, win cigarettes from the fellows over here and then leave again. No one plays for money. Cigarettes are worth more than gold down here. . . .

Weather much clearer, temperature 57° below but no wind. Everything is so still outside that we almost wonder whether there is any civilization in the world outside our own right here. George Tennant went for a walk and when he wanted to come in, could not find the entrance to the house. He kept walking round and around the radio towers, and only found it by falling into it. George was plenty cold and decided not to take another walk for awhile. . . .

There are many different kinds of work going on. De Ganahl is sewing a dog whip; June is making a sun compass; Smith is writing his diary; Roth is patching his shirt; Vaughan and Thorne are sewing up a dog that was nearly torn to pieces in a fight; Paul Siple is making a lamp; Chips is doing carpenter work; Tennant is reading and cooking at the same time; and I am sewing a piece of canvas for a bunk cover. I am also experimenting on a pair of boots with canvas legs and tongues and sealskin soles. We are all beginning to think about the trail, the plans for spring, the polar plane flight, and starting to get ready for these things.

Now I am scheduled to go on mess for a week. This means keeping the box full of coal and washing dishes for 42 men, and all the pots and pans that go with it. No man is sorry when the week is up. . . .

It is Pete Demas' turn as night watchman. At 5:00 A.M. he rushed into the Edgar Barratt House all out of breath, and in much confusion said that there was a crack in the Barrier between the two houses—the Barrier was breaking off. The fellows got out of their sleeping bags so fast that the caribou hairs from the bags had no chance to cling to them. Usually, they are covered with them. Most of them were headed for the door in less than a second, when on regular mornings the watchman has to call three times, and it takes an hour to dress, puffing and blowing the whole time. Few stopped to put on clothing or boots, though some scrambled for pants and one said, "Where in hell is my cap?" No one thought about freezing to death, half dressed in the subzero temperature. No one thought about the cutting wind that would pierce the body like a knife. No one thought of the foolhardiness of any attempt to escape when there was no escape. Their brains were a blank, and they acted like automatons.

Everyone was speechless, forgetting even to rouse the heavy sleepers who had not awakened. Our radio operator, Hanson, rushed around trying to get together an emergency set, a transmitter, pliers, screwdrivers, and other equipment. I think the first men through the door were "Cyclone" Billy Haines and Russ Owens, who had feared this from the moment we set foot on the Barrier. Billy went out with his flashlight, shining it all around looking for the crack. Meanwhile, Pete Demas went over to the Roswell Barratt House and calmly started to build the fire there. When he came out he met Billy and asked him what he was doing. Billy, all excited, said, "Where is the crack?" Pete laughed. There was no crack. The joke was planned for the benefit of Russ, who was always talking about the Barrier breaking off. The other fellows who had fallen for it were almost ashamed to come over for breakfast in the Roswell House. . . .

The temperature fell to 71° below, and that is cold. Our breath froze as soon as we went outside; it sounded like the ruffling of tissue paper. The radio party was all set to go out and test radio waves, so the dogs were taken out of the tunnel and put in harness. In a few minutes they began to draw up and freeze, so they were hurried back in the tunnel again. Hanson then decided to man-haul the sled a few miles and I volunteered to go along. Hanson, Joe de Ganahl, and I started off and went about four miles, using a compass and flashlight to find our way. We set our course by sighting on a star ahead and then going straight for it. We laid down flags to mark our trail, but on our way back we could not even see the flags. As soon as we broke out over the Barrier we saw the beacon light on the radio tower and also the beam of a flashlight. It was Commander Byrd flashing his light for us from the Administration Building. Night or day his mind was never off the men who were out on a trail. . . .

Today Blackburn took a bath. Quin seems to like taking baths down here, about once every two weeks, though most of the fellows haven't bothered about it; it is too much work melting snow to make water. But Quin will bring in the big wash pan and after everyone retires to his bunk you can hear water splashing and Quin grunting. He will say, "Egad, it is pretty cold, but this warm water sure feels good." One night Quin got in the rubber bathtub. He had just curled up in it with his knees touching his chin when someone came in with some snow and dumped it on him. Quin gave such a leap that the tub flopped and most of the water he had taken such pains melting snow for started running all over the floor. A bucket of snow makes less than a quarter of a bucket of water. . . .

We are having some wonderful moonlight days and nights; they are gorgeous and make things more pleasant for us during these months of darkness.

There is a halo around the moon tonight, and stars twinkle in the frosty atmosphere. It is 68° below and going down. We make up rations and get ready for the trail again. . . .

The temperature has dropped to 72° below, our record for the year so far. Although it is cold, I took a walk with St. Lunaire and three pups down the bay, as far as the pressure ridges. There was a corona around the moon, three rings of different colors, green, pink, and yellow. . . .

Today is the day of the beautiful morning. It is August 20 and we saw the sun for the first time since April 19. It came up over the horizon as if just taking a peek at us for a few moments and then ducked down again. Some of the fellows climbed up the radio towers to catch a longer glimpse of the great sight. Others put on their skis and skied for the Barrier. Chris Braathen and I harnessed up our dogs and started for the bay ice out in the Bay of Whales. We killed a seal there and pelted him on the spot, hauling him in for fresh meat for our dogs. . . .

7

THE Antarctic night was over. We celebrated the return of the sun by hoisting the flags of three nations—Great Britain and Norway, in memory of Captain Scott and Roald Amundsen, and our own, the proud insignia of our base at Little America.

Now the lengthening days would be busy ones, getting ready for the trail. There was tremendous rivalry between the snowmobile crew and the dog drivers. The snowmobile had done excellent work around the base and in hauling supplies for short distances, but I had no faith in it for trail work and I don't think Commander Byrd did, either.

Shackleton, Scott, and Mawson had dreamed of the great help that machines would be to them. Shackleton experimented with rubber tires and coglike treads on an automobile with an air-cooled four-cylinder engine, but got only a few miles with it. Mawson's motorized sledge, with propeller attachment, failed also. Scott had three motorized sledges—one was lost through the ice in unloading and the other two broke down soon after they were put to use. Commander Byrd was under no illusions regarding motorized surface equipment on our first expedition. Yet he, too, experimented because he felt that mechanized transport would one day be developed as the next great step in Antarctic exploration. But he never thought of depending entirely on tractors and snowmobiles. He knew that the Eskimo dog was the only reliable means of polar exploration, because dog teams can go where planes can't land and where it is impossible for tractors to travel.

However, the Commander took along a Ford snowmobile with caterpillar treads, and the snowmobile crew vowed they would conquer the Barrier. They had done work equivalent to that of several dog teams in hauling supplies from the Barrier cache to a safer position. Now they were anxious to prove the vehicle's worth on the trail by following us on a 200-mile advance trail-blazing trek through a dangerously crevassed area leading to the Queen Maud Range of mountains.

The trip's purpose was both to blaze the trail and to provide a supporting party for the Geological Party that would follow. We were also to serve as a rescue party in case of accident to the polar flight in preparation. It was our mission to erect beacons and caches of emergency supplies every fifty miles.

There were four of us in the supporting party, with three dog teams of nine dogs each, pulling sleds that groaned beneath a burden of a thousand pounds. The snowmobile was to follow us, towing three sledges loaded with supplies for the Geological Party. Arthur Walden, Chris Braathen, Joe de Ganahl, and I were only awaiting favorable weather to get started. This came on October 15.

As we hitched up our dogs and made a last inspection of our sleds, Commander Byrd stood by watching us, anxious that all precautions humanly possible should be taken for our safety.

"Boys," he said, "I would rather never fly over the South Pole than to lose one of you. Always take the course of safety; your lives are precious to me."

The dogs were excited and eager to get going; St. Lunaire

especially, as if he seemed to realize his responsibility in leading the party.

"Yath!" I called, and off he went with the other dogs following, all straining in their harnesses.

They didn't make the speed that their spirits and the temperature called for, however. The loads were heavy and they were not yet used to the steady grind of pulling, so for four days we rested them often.

The thermometer dropped past 40° below zero. The snow was like sand, and the heavily loaded sleds bogged down in drifts through which the dogs could not pull them. We harnessed ourselves with the dogs and pulled with them, but were forced to rest every few hundred yards. Often it took us an hour to make a mile of progress. After four days of this, it was evident that we could not go on without lightening our loads. The Geological Party turned back and we, the supporting party of the South Polar flight, struggled on after caching everything we could possibly do without on our journey. The Geological Party would have to reorganize their loads and plans before they could follow us.

A blizzard blew down and raged all the fifth day, making it impossible to go on. To keep warm, we stayed in our sleeping bags, crawling out only to eat. The rest of the time we just lay there listening to the tent rattle as if the canvas were made of metal.

The dogs had worked hard and willingly, and could well use the day of rest. Huskies sleep snugly through the worst storms because they dig a shelter of snow about themselves, and just let the drifting snow pile over them.

After the storm a heavy fog settled over us, but we had to move in spite of limited visibility because each day counted immeasurably. We expected to come to the worst crevassed area of the Barrier that day—the place where Roald Amundsen nearly came to grief on his historic dash to the South Pole and which he called "The Trap."

We made only twenty miles before we were forced to camp in another blizzard. This one kept us in our tent for two days, and when it cleared we could see two large "haycocks" some distance ahead of us. A haycock is a large pyramidal mound of ice and snow over a vent hole in a crevasse, and is always a sign of hidden danger.

Fully prepared for emergencies, therefore, we traveled in two units. We four men were roped together as one, the three teams were the second. In this way if a man, sled, or team of dogs should break through a crevasse, help would be at hand.

Except for the speed of the dogs, it was impossible to tell whether we were going uphill or down. A thick and choking fog gathered us into its breathless embrace, blinding our vision to the dangers ahead of us and stirring the first touch of fear in our hearts towards an enemy we could not fight. We struggled on as best we could until at last, to our great relief, the mist lifted to reveal the way ahead.

Chris Braathen complained that he had something in his eye, and that it was bothering the life out of him. I looked in his eye carefully, but could find nothing.

"Chris," I said, "I think you are becoming snowblind."

It was the beginning of this painful malady for all of us. Although we put on our snow glasses, they did not ease the flaming hot pain. Arthur Walden had the best pair of glasses in the party which he insisted I wear because I was leading the teams. I shall always be grateful to him for this sacrifice, for I know his eyes were just as sore as mine.

We had to depend on our dogs to guide us, and St. Lunaire proved his worth as a lead dog. It is the usual custom of a driver

to go ahead of his team and guide the way over dangerous areas.
A lead dog does not always obey the moment he is spoken to,
and one second of delay may be fatal. But St. Lunaire obeyed
my commands so promptly and accurately that I never found it
necessary to go ahead of him during the whole trip into Antarctica's most dangerous area.

I had to keep my aching, burning eyes constantly on the
trail watching for pitfalls. We crossed chasm after chasm until
we were finally surrounded completely by treacherous haycocks
and crevasses. Realizing we were in a bad spot, we called a halt
to decide what to do.

Walden, de Ganahl, and I skied ahead for a hundred yards
and found an opening which we thought we might be able to go
through. We set out again, but we had gone only little further
on when I suddenly saw a huge, black hole right ahead of me.

St. Lunaire instantly obeyed my frantic command to turn,
but he was so near the hole that the sled in passing came alongside the very edge of it.

To the right of this pit was a haycock concealing an opening in the Barrier large enough to swallow us all in one gulp. I
hurried the dogs between the chasm and the haycock, urging
them on for fear they might stop. If my team halted, the others
would also have to stop, which might plunge them down the
incline into the abyss we had just avoided.

No sooner had we got through to what we thought was a
safe place than we ran into another gaping crevasse. Here we all
stopped. Every inch of travel was carrying us deeper and deeper
into a wilderness of haycocks, open chasms, and crevasses. There
was only a tiny space available in which to turn the teams
around, and every sled tipped over in the process. We scrambled
like mad to right them again. The area was all hollow beneath
our feet. Portions of the Barrier kept dropping with a cannon-

like booming that made our spines creep as we skimmed over it. What chance would the snowmobile have? We were lucky to get out of it alive on skis with the dogs and our heavy sleds.

We were worn out, so we camped, but sleep was impossible. The moaning, roaring, and cracking of the splitting and shifting ice on which we lay made continual thunderous noises as the Barrier settled beneath us, collapsing somewhere in its depths. My weary eyes would close and then snap open again, as I expected any moment that the ice would open up beneath our tent. It did under Walden and Braathen's, but the crack was narrow and they did not fall through.

I got half out of my sleeping bag to turn the generator on the radio for Joe de Ganahl while he sent the following report of our situation to Commander Byrd, a copy of which I inscribed in my diary:

The peaceful Barrier showed its sternest front today when the monotony of 160 miles of unexciting sledging was broken by our efforts to penetrate the maze of crevasses, covered chasms, and hollow haycocks eleven miles south of Depot 3.

The tents were pitched tonight between two pitfalls three miles east of the scene of our escape from whatever is below the countless hollow crusts over which we passed. The Barrier trembles and roars occasionally as new traps open in this area where the pressure of the ice is equalized.

From 81° South this morning a long line of knolls, jagged peaks, and rolling domes glistened majestically on the crest of a hilltop stretching east and west. We had gone five miles when Bursey, who was leading the roped caravan, swung his sled to a halt. His dogs were on the roof of a round, hollow pit 50 feet in diameter.

There were many such invisible caverns on the ascent of the hill, some filled, some bridged with snow, evidently craters of haycocks opened by released pressure.

Soon crevasses, a few open, some filled, most roofed, crossed our path. Five miles of dodging and rushing brought us to a stop. To the south and west were graceful domes, fantastic peaks, and black shadows—ugly and forbidding lines of upheaved ice. To the east, a deep valley was crossed and recrossed by scores of the gray depressions we had learned to respect.

Well-roped, we planned a short reconnaissance on foot. Walden stepped away from his sled into a crevasse and sank down to his waist. He was pulled out again and went down into a second. We reached the hilltop ridge running southwest between villages of haycocks. We proceeded with the teams. In five minutes we were shut in by hollow domes, every step on a thin, trembling roof. We crossed a safe-looking ridge and slid down ten feet from an open hole with blackness for a bottom, and turned the teams to the west. Bursey slipped over the brink of a pit as we crossed a narrow bridge between it and haycocks, but the rope dragged him back. There was a 100-foot hole to the left and countless haycocks to the right.

We followed a narrow highway west until a wide, thinly covered crevasse blocked our path to the hopeless area ahead. There was no room to turn teams between haycocks. Braathen, roped and on skis, tested the largest and we rushed the dogs around and over the dome to retrace our steps a few hundred yards. Bursey stopped to fix a harness and the surface sank under Braathen's sled. The teams were hurried forward and pulled him to a thicker roof. The route flag slipped through into space. Below everything was hollow. We tried a valley with many crevasses, but Braathen's experience and short dodges brought us safe around. All believe we will find a way through to the east.

—DE GANAHL

Walden reported to Commander Byrd, "Believe it fatal for snowmobile to proceed beyond 81°. No imagination can picture conditions due south of Depot No. 3. Our position dead reckoning Lat. 81° 11′ South, Long. 163° 25′ West."

In reply to this, Commander Byrd instructed us to go back to the beginning of the bad area and leave messages for the snowmobile party that was following our trail. If they got that far they were to be told not to go beyond, and to return to the base as soon as possible.

So Braathen and I took a sled and my team of dogs, and drove back seven miles to where we had met the first crevasse. There we stuck up eight flags across our trail, with a note tied in the center containing the Commander's orders. We laid bets, however, that the snowmobile would not get that far.

After we got back to the camp, Joe de Ganahl joined us and we started out on skis to try picking our way through to the east, leaving Walden with the teams. It took us four hours to pick our way two miles, but before we returned we laid down seventy-five flags to mark the zigzag trail. We were gone so long that Walden became worried.

Although it was evening and we were pretty tired, we thought it best to drive right through at once, as we had only a ski track and our flags to follow. If visibility should become poor, they would be of little help to us. As long as the weather was clear we were not deterred by the hour, for we were getting twenty-four hours of daylight again. I told the others that St. Lunaire could be depended on to take us through.

But as we started to penetrate the mass of broken-up ice, I knew that this was the supreme test for both of us. With the flags to guide me, I gave St. Lunaire the word when to turn right or left, and he never faltered. At times the snow would drop beneath us as we skied alongside the sleds with one hand on the gee-pole.

Several of the dogs fell into a crevasse and were pulled out again by the others who kept going. Part of the time we ran between open chasms, only a few feet from the edges. Then we sped along the sides of a steep incline, sliding toward a black pit at the bottom of it. If St. Lunaire had made one mistake it might have been fatal for us.

When we finally reached safe territory and looked back, thankful to be alive and uninjured, we were awe-stricken at the thought of what might have happened if we had delayed our passage and the fog had closed in on us in the middle of it.

De Ganahl reported to Commander Byrd, "Great upheavals have taken place here since Amundsen's time. Nothing he describes can compare with it."

One more day brought us to our objective, two hundred miles south of Little America. We built our last depot at 81° 45′ South, 163° 35′ West, and cached six hundred pounds of supplies, marking the depot with flags running east and west for two miles on either side. We built a beacon out of snow blocks and planted on the top the Stars and Stripes of my then newly adopted country. We were conscious of the proud distinction of carrying the American flag farther south than it had ever been before.

On the return journey dangers still lurked at every turn, and dark, sullen days made poor visibility; but the way was marked, and St. Lunaire followed the old trail without a great deal of difficulty.

There was no way of avoiding the awful mess of chasms, haycocks, and crevasses that we now called "Chasm Pass," but luckily we made good progress with only a few bad moments. At one point St. Lunaire suddenly disappeared completely. Fortunately the rest of the team stopped instantly. I unhooked my safety belt and skied forward. Luny had dropped into a crevasse that was thinly bridged over. Inching up to it on my stomach, I could see him hanging by his trace, attached to the gang-line. I hauled him out with a feeling of relief matched only by his gratitude. He wagged his tail and tried to lick my face, but I hugged him as a sort of compromise.

When we were about seventy-five miles from Little America, we saw a black object ahead of us. As we drew near to it we saw that it was the snowmobile, broken down and abandoned. The men had walked back, hauling a sled themselves, and we found out afterwards it had taken them eight days to make it.

When we got back, the whole gang at Little America was waiting to welcome us. The happiest face was that of Commander Byrd, who was the first to greet and congratulate us. We had, he said, done the best and most important work of the expedition. By blazing the trail and establishing caches of emergency supplies, we had made possible the spring work of the Geological Party and the safety support of the forthcoming polar flight.

And St. Lunaire, the rejected and sorry-looking "leftover" who had adopted me as his master, had earned his reputation as the finest lead dog in Little America, Antarctica.

8

MY dream had come true. The thing I had visualized as a boy, driving my team of dogs in the north of Newfoundland, was at last a reality. I had helped to prove the worth of Eskimo dogs in the Great White South of Scott and Amundsen. Now it was the turn of Commander Byrd, who had given me this chance. He too had a dream—to fly over the South Pole as he had over the North Pole—and its successful fulfillment would be the dramatic climax of the entire expedition. The scientific investigations, the geological and geographical surveys, the discovery and investigation of new lands and mountains to the east of Little America were all undoubtedly of greater importance. The South Pole had been discovered. Men had been there. Yet the first flight by air over the bottom of the world held a dramatic appeal which took the fancy of not only all the men on the expedition but of all the world that waited for its outcome.

At Little America great preparations had been made all through the year for this event. Every man in camp had a hand in it, because it symbolized success for the expedition and every member of it. We dog men had done what we could by blazing the 200-mile trail and building a beacon of emergency supplies. Now we stood ready to rush to the rescue should something happen to force a landing on the polar plateau or in the mountains.

Commander Byrd himself was very humble about his role on the flight. Should it prove successful, Bernt Balchen and Harold June, the pilots, would deserve the credit for having accomplished it, while Captain McKinley would take the essential photographs to document the achievement. I know that when the question arose whether the three-motored plane was capable of gaining the necessary altitude and sustaining its flight for eight hundred miles and back with four passengers, Commander Byrd would have stayed at the base himself except for one consideration. There was not a man in camp who would not have given his right arm to go on that flight, or, as the Commander said, would not have been entitled to go if there had been room. But, at the most, only one could go. We all wanted Commander Byrd to be that one. It was his dream, he had worked harder than anyone to make it possible, and he was entitled to the fulfillment of it. It would have been unthinkable to the rest of us that he should not personally make this historic flight. Through his eyes we would see those mountains towering 14,000 feet above sea level and the great polar plateau beyond them, the eternal wilderness of snow and glacial rivers of ice which now buried a once-tropical land.

Day after day Billy Haines, our chief weatherman, would come in and make his report to Commander Byrd after watching for hours at a time colored balloons ascend into the frosty atmosphere. "Not today," he would say. "This is not the day." Billy had been with Commander Byrd before, in the Arctic, and the Commander trusted implicitly in his judgment. When Billy gave the word to go, that would be good enough for him.

All of us at Little America put great faith in Billy's ability to forecast the weather; he had always been right. No man could read the sky and make deductions like Billy could. He could tell every hour in the day what the weather would be, and he made no mistakes about it. If he wasn't sure, he said nothing.

The polar plane was tested, examined, and re-examined day after day by three expert mechanics. Nothing was left to chance. A preliminary flight was made over our trail to lay a base at the foot of the Queen Maud Range. Everything was in readiness for the polar flight.

The morning of November 28, 1929, Thanksgiving Day, looked bright and clear at Little America. The temperature was 15° above zero. Everyone held his breath for the answer which only one man in camp could give.

Billy stood watching the wind vane slowly spinning, looking first to the north where the sky was cloudy, then to the south which was clear except for a few little cirrus clouds.

Inside someone said, "Here comes Bill. We will soon know the answer."

Billy, a smile on his face, went straight to the Commander without a word.

"Yes, this is your day," he said.

The camp jumped to life. The blowtorch was turned on full force to heat up the engines. The motor oil was heated to the boiling point over a fire made from a gasoline barrel. The gear was stored in the plane—sleeping bags, skis, food, tent, and a little sled to man-haul in case the plane was damaged. But no one thought seriously of this possibility. With such organization and forethought, the Commander could not lose.

The mechanics began pouring the boiling oil into the engines. The tanks were filled to running over with gasoline. The crank was set into position to wind her up. A cry of "Contact!" was called and repeated. Then there was a roar as the three engines came to life and started to purr. Balchen at the controls, dressed in his furs and ready to go, tested each engine separately, gunning them at intervals to warm them up for the take-off. Harold June, copilot and radioman, was testing the radio. Ashley McKinley was maneuvering his aerial camera into position for the continuous moving picture he would take on one side going to the Pole, and on the other side coming back.

Everything was in readiness. Commander Byrd was giving his last instructions to the camp. He shook hands with each one of us as every man wished him luck, then crawled up into the plane and closed the door behind him. Balchen began to rev the engines up and the plane moved slowly forward on her landing skis. He taxied to the far end of the field where he would have a downgrade take-off.

We all watched as Balchen gave her the gun. Would he be able to get her in the air, or was she too heavy? The engines had a mighty load to lift.

One man held a watch to mark the time the skis cleared the snow. We stood in silence as the *Floyd Bennett* came streaking down the runway past us, suddenly took hold, and with a lift began soaring upward.

"She's off!" came the shout. It was 3:29 P.M.

We threw our caps in the air, slapped each other on the back, and yelled at the top of our voices. We watched the plane until it was out of sight, then slowly walked toward the radio shack where we could listen to the hum of the motors in the loud-speaker. If anything went wrong we would hear it there. If the engines died, or so much as coughed, we would know it instantly.

The tense moments lengthened into hours, but the steady roaring of the engines in the loud-speaker never faltered. Toward midnight there was a new tenseness among the listeners. We knew the plane was getting close to the Pole.

We were all waiting for the crucial word that would crown all our labors and our great adventure.

Suddenly Harold June broke through the humming of the engines with the following radio message: "My calculations indicate that we have reached the vicinity of the South Pole. Flying high for a survey. Byrd."

Within a few minutes after that message was given out, at 1:30 A.M. Greenwich Civil Time, presses started running all over the world. In many places the story was already set in type, awaiting confirmation: "Byrd has flown over the South Pole."

The expedition was a success. But nothing could relieve our tension until the plane landed safely at Little America. Clouds were gathering in the south and anything might still happen to send us racing with our dogs for the emergency base two hundred miles away at the Queen Maud mountains.

My pulse skipped a beat, and I am sure that of others did also, when the engines in the loud-speaker suddenly stopped roaring. It was nearly five o'clock in the morning. What had happened? Had they been forced to make an emergency landing, or had the engines stopped running at a high altitude? Nothing came over the radio. By six o'clock we understood the silence when we heard the roaring of the engines again. They had run low on gas and had stopped to refuel at the emergency cache at the Queen Maud Range.

A little over three hours later we sighted the plane coming down from the south, a little dot on the horizon. Van der Veer, the Paramount movie man, had his camera all ready to get a picture of this triumphant landing. At eight minutes after ten o'clock, eighteen hours and thirty-nine minutes after her take-off, her skis struck the snow at Little America.

Beginning with Commander Byrd, one by one the four men were hauled out of the plane and carried to the Mess Hall on our shoulders. Paul Siple and I staggered in with Bernt Balchen, who was no light-weight. The men were all deaf from the roaring of the engines and could not hear even our wild shouting. They were so tired and sleepy that all they could do was laugh with us. We celebrated a belated Thanksgiving for two days, the most riotously happy bunch of men that ever made history.

part III

THE LONG MARCH

*U.S. Antarctic Service
Expedition / 1939–41*

1

WHEN we left Little America I in February of 1930, most of the men, I think, did so gladly; but a few of us felt a strange, sad twinge of reluctance.

Commander Byrd said to "Cyclone" Billy Haines, our meteorologist, "We'll be back, Bill."

"Not me," said Billy, who had been with Byrd on his North Pole expedition. "Once is quite enough."

But Antarctica had gotten into Billy's blood too, though he did not know it then. Four years later Commander Byrd watched him digging furiously down through the snow and ice to our old quarters at Little America I; and to my great regret I was not with them.

Our Commander was now Admiral Byrd, and his appointment on the retired list was a result of the public demand for his promotion and his refusal to accept an appointment over the heads of fellow officers on the active lists. He had refused to allow Congress to promote him to the rank of Admiral in recognition of his North Pole flight. And when Congress decided to vote him a special medal of honor after his South Pole flight, he asked that medals be given to his men instead. In response to this request, Congress broke all precedents by voting medals for every man who had been on the expedition. To each of us Admiral Byrd wrote a personal letter, and the one he wrote to me is one of my most valued possessions:

MY DEAR JACK:

It is with delight that I present to you this Congressional Medal.

You gave many months of your life towards making our expedition successful. Now that a year has passed since we have returned home, I want you to know that my gratitude to you is as firm as ever—that throughout our lives whatever may be our various fortunes you will find that my appreciation will not grow less.

The time that has elapsed has only increased the respect of our countrymen for our expedition. May the years ahead have the same effect.

The expression of this respect is this medal which is knighthood that your grateful countrymen have conferred upon you—the highest honor within their gift. This is a recognition that will carry your name on the pages of history.

On the face of the medal there is mention of the expedition's material accomplishments, but what it represents in an even deeper sense is that which has been invisible, which cannot be described—the spirit of our expedition.

It is internal bitterness caused by fame, ambition, money and jealousy which, after the return home, has destroyed the spirit of most past expeditions. You have not let these things touch you, and so I congratulate you and am grateful to you in a double sense. It is often more difficult to keep our sense of balance and proportion in civilization than in the polar regions.

It is my confident hope that this spirit will live as a bright page in history.

In conclusion, I want to say that whenever you come my way, you will receive a warm welcome and the hand of friendship.

Your friend,

R. E. BYRD

On our homeward journey Commander Byrd had written in his diary, "The mission is done, and well, I hope. . . . I hope it sincerely, principally for these men who have gone each step of the way with me. They have given two years of their lives to the service of science, a hard and grudging master, and it would be a pity if their sacrifice were neither understood nor appreciated."

But the world did recognize the value of the first Byrd Antarctic Expedition, both in its execution and its achievement. Geographical, geological, and meteorological discoveries had been dramatically extended beyond any previous knowledge. As Dr. Hayes summed up: "Admiral Byrd . . . went out to Antarctica for information and he got it. . . . He is to be congratulated on his splendid achievements, not the least of which, with his huge personnel, was the fact of not losing a single life." And Admiral Byrd refused to accept congratulations or honors that he could not share with his men. Also, he refused to exaggerate the importance of his achievements.

In closing the account of his first expedition (described in his book *Little America*), he stated his wish "to put an end, once and for all, to the journalistic practice of referring to our efforts as the 'conquest' of the Antarctic. The Antarctic has not been conquered. At best we simply tore away a bit more of the veil which conceals its secrets. An immense job yet remains to be done. The Antarctic will yield to no single expedition, nor yet to half a dozen. In its larger aspects, it still remains, and will probably remain for many years to come, one of the great *undone* tasks of the world."

In 1934 Admiral Byrd returned to carry on with this task. The reason I was not among his helpers to contribute my small part in this continuation of his efforts was that I was off on another adventure of my own.

It began on the *City of New York,* the old *Samson* from Norway, when that South Polar ship of our first expedition was on exhibition at the 1933 Century of Progress Exposition in Chicago. Many people came to see this relic of the Antarctic, and I was one who took them through the ship, telling them of her history and of our adventures in Antarctica. Among these visitors was a girl from Michigan whose name was Ada deGraff.

Does anyone know how these things happen? I don't. I dated Ada once, and then she had to go home; but we corresponded. After the Fair I was working on a Great Lakes ship and Ada came to see me once when we docked at a port in Michigan. She swiped a dish that had pictures of the ship on it, and that was when I first learned that she loved, and liked to collect, historic dishes.

The third time I saw her I put a ring on her finger, and the following spring, in 1934, we were married.

Then after our daughter Gloria was born I sledged with dogs in the Adirondack Mountains. Ada and Glory were with me, and so was my old lead dog, St. Lunaire, who lived out his life with us as a reward for his faithful service in Antarctica.

But as time went on, the lure of the Great White South again became too much for me. In 1939 I asked to be included as a member of the U.S. Antarctic Service Expedition; I could no longer resist the urge within me. I had to go back, though there was not quite the same excitement about it. I was not setting forth into the unknown, but returning with the quiet inevitability of fate to my first great love. And to her everlasting credit, Ada understood this. She even went to work so that I could do it. But in her was the origin of a sobering difference which I was soon to discover. I now had a wife and a small daughter to leave behind me; and I was to learn the full meaning of the Antarctic night to men who are not immune, as I had been in my youth, to the ties and comforts of home and civilization.

Ada's parting gift to me was a fine movie camera and film. Little Gloria parted with her pet Siberian husky, Gray Cloud, whom I had raised from a puppy for her, as her contribution to the cause of South Polar exploration, and "so you won't get too lonely, Daddy. Gray Cloud is the only one of us who can go with you." I little dreamed then what a comfort Gray Cloud would be to me during the long months of darkness buried under the drifting snow with a blizzard howling and the vast distance which separated me from those I loved clutching at the pit of my stomach. This was something I had not experienced at Little America I.

It was September 21, 1939, when I received instructions from the Department of the Interior, Washington, D.C., to report for duty with the U.S. Antarctic Service. I was ordered to proceed to Wonalancet, New Hampshire, where the Eskimo dogs were being trained and conditioned for the long trip across the Pacific Ocean and the hard grind of unloading the ship on the Barrier.

When the beautiful little Gray Cloud and I arrived at the Seeley Kennels, there were dogs on chains wherever we looked. One hundred fifty had already been collected and forty more were on the way in from Alaska. Besides the Siberian huskies and the larger Eskimo huskies, we had Malamutes and a team of huge wolf dogs. They were all so excited and full of life that it took two men to put a dog in harness and prevent a tangle that might end in a fight to a finish. It was going to take time and patience to train new dogs.

I chained Gray Cloud to a tree so that he might get used to the other dogs and to the idea that he must take his place with them, under the same conditions. I told him, in the way we had of understanding one another, that he must learn to defend himself, for his life would be a hard one. There was no place for a weakling, and in the Great Unknown, our lives would depend on each other.

We had men as well as dogs to train. Many of the younger men, and even some of the older ones, had never seen an Eskimo dog or any kind of a husky before. They had been sent to the kennels to work with the dogs, to learn to know them and how to drive them. So day in and day out we worked on the dogs together, driving them, matching them up in teams, breaking in lead dogs, working on harnesses, gang-lines, dog crates, and many other things that are so vital to the success of a polar expedition.

With our sailing deadline reached, I was ordered to report to one of the expedition's ships, the U.S.S. *Bear,* sixty-eight-year old veteran of many a rough and icy sea. As I had had experience in fore-and-aft and square-rigged vessels, and possessed a third officer's ticket, I was asked to rig her out as a barkentine and go on the trip south as sail master.

On November 15 the expedition's other ship, the *North Star,* carrying sixty-four of the dogs, pulled out, bound for Philadelphia to take on a plane. And on the morning of the twenty-second we slipped our lines in a rousing snowstorm — a good send-off for the old ship *Bear* starting out on a polar voyage.

We were off at last, this time under government sponsorship to continue the Antarctic studies headed by Admiral Byrd. The purpose of the expedition was to map the coast line and interior sections of Byrd's discoveries, and to establish a magnetic station, a seismograph station to record earthquake disturbances, and a weather station. Cosmic ray observations would also be made up to altitudes of 25,000 feet. All these observations, correlated with data obtained in the temperate zones, were expected to prove valuable in weather forecasting. The mapping was to be done by means of aerial photography supplemented by basic ground survey. After the long Antarctic night was over, it would be my job, with the help of Dick Moulton, another dog-team driver, to transport the surveyor, Leonard Berlin, to the Hal Flood mountains (now known as Hal Flood Range), a round trip of 1,220 miles. Here we would plant the United States flag where no men had ever been before. It would be the longest dog-team trip of my life, and I was looking forward to it.

2

WHEN sailing through smooth water with all sails set to help the engine, we made good time. With the rig of a barkentine, the *Bear* had square sails on the foremast and fore-and-half rig on the main and mizzen; but we could carry no sail on her mainmast because we had an airplane loaded on deck just back of it. This was comparatively little canvas, but it helped a good deal in steadying the ship when we hit rough weather, for the old *Bear* could roll like the *Eleanor Bolling,* "the Evermore Rolling" of our first expedition.

It was a long trip at best, and the details would be as monotonous as many of our days over that great southern stretch of the Pacific with not a sight of even a bird, whale, sail, or fish — just the same routine day in and day out, setting sails and taking them in; bracing the yards first on the starboard side and then on the port side. For days our only diversion was provided by an albatross which followed us, becoming such a familiar figure that we named him "Mike." But the "Roaring Fifties" gave our minds something to think about, and gave the old *Bear* a worse beating than the Forties had done.

When we started passing icebergs and the water smoothed out, I knew we must be drawing near the ice pack. I went aloft for a better view, and there it was—the great Antarctic ice pack extending east and west for as far as I could see.

On New Year's Day we ran west along the pack and then due north again, trying to get around a tongue of it. A seal came up by a pan of ice, the first we had seen, and I counted five whales and 170 icebergs as we sailed through the Devil's Graveyard on January 2, 1940. Some of the bergs were tabular in shape and others looked like old forts or big castles.

We were still hoping to get to the Bay of Whales before the *North Star,* which was only two hundred miles south of Dunedin, New Zealand. We had come straight from Panama, while the *North Star* had broken her trip by stopping at Pitcairn and Rapper islands, as well as at both Wellington and Dunedin. But here we were, picking our way through little pieces of ice no bigger than a seal's head, afraid to let this great icebreaker called the *Bear*—this ship that had weathered gales in the worst seas on earth, and had for years plowed her way through Arctic and Antarctic ice packs—touch one of them for fear of knocking a hole in her!

We could have cut off many miles by just pushing through the scattered ice along by the tongue and side of the pack, but Ben Johanson, the ice pilot, was not scheduled to take over full responsibility until we entered the pack at the 180th meridian, bound for the Ross Sea.

Ben had seen much of the southern and northern packs, and he knew ice, as I did, from childhood. Over and over again Ben grumbled at the Navy boys, "Well, if you fellows are afraid of a little ice like this, you will never get to the Bay of Whales!" And meanwhile we lost our "race," for the *North Star* was through the pack and in the Ross Sea before we even entered the ice.

At last, however, Captain Ben took over and we steamed

into the pack. I got a great kick out of watching our crew of young Navy boys as Ben made the *Bear* shiver in every timber, ramming and stopping dead, then ramming again until, with engines full speed ahead, she would plow her way through the thickening ice.

On the eleventh of January we pulled through to clear water in the Ross Sea. Antarctic petrels flew over the fringes of the pack, sometimes landing on pieces of ice and then flying away again as the ship bore down on them. And somehow these little snowy petrels began to generate the atmosphere of another world . . . but it was like returning home to me. I started packing my things so I would lose no time in getting off the *Bear* when we landed. We knew by radio that the *North Star* was already unloading. We even put on the wings of the Admiral's plane so it would be all ready to fly as soon as we arrived at Little America.

We steamed into the Bay of Whales on January 14, 1940, and brought the *Bear* alongside the ice just ahead of the *North Star*. We were over the bowsprit and onto the bay ice as soon as the ship touched it, stretching our legs and bantering with the boys from the *Star* who ran to meet us.

First to be unloaded were the dogs, and we lost no time about it for the trip had been hard on them and some had been very sick. But now, with their harnesses on, they were turned loose and they ran back and forth and around in circles, rolling and raising a terrific din for the sheer joy of it. From now on we could not have done without them.

True, we had tractors, but almost the first thing one of them did was to go into a crevasse—fortunately not a big one, so after shoveling for hours we finally got the tractor out. I was all in when I crawled into my sleeping bag in a little tent on top of the Barrier and slept the full twelve hours.

When I awoke, a low drift was coming in with a strong wind. My clothes were cold and my boots were frozen so stiff I had to work them with my hands for some time before I could squeeze my feet into them. I put on my skis and raced down over the Barrier to the *North Star* for breakfast and warmth. I was no sooner on board than we all heard a tremendous noise. The Barrier started breaking off, and tons of ice came rolling and rumbling toward the *Star.* Lines were cut at once, and we floated out in the bay without damage, the *Bear* following suit. A few hours later we were again tied up and once more supplies started coming out of the hold. The unloading went on twenty-four hours a day, in continual sunlight, with every man on a twelve-hour watch.

Our trail led over the bay ice for a short distance, and then up over the Barrier. Near the top was a small crevasse where we had to watch our step, and from there we hauled to a food cache at a safe distance.

Some of the dog drivers were pretty green at the game of driving dogs, and their dogs were running all over with them. One of them was heading back to the ship after unloading at the cache when his lead dog went straight for that part of the Barrier which had broken off. When the driver shouted at them, the dogs only increased their speed, but they were saved from running off the edge of the Barrier by falling down a crevasse. The driver rolled off his sled just in time as the team and sled disappeared.

We all thought the team was done for, but luckily the sled had caught three feet down, wedging itself in the crevasse. Below that, the nine dogs were all hanging on the gang-line in their harnesses, and we were able to rescue them. A rope was fastened around Dick Moulton's waist and he was lowered into the crevasse where he sent up each dog fastened to a second rope. To our great relief, all the dogs were saved.

Admiral Byrd was off in the *Bear* exploring the waters to eastward while we finished unloading the *North Star*. The Captain was in a great hurry to get away, and when the *North Star* pulled out, bound for Valparaiso, we didn't even have a place to cook a meal as only two small tents were up. So the first thing we did was to put up a cook tent and a sleeping tent at West Base (Little America III), which was six or seven miles from Little America I and II, and only two miles from our Barrier cache. This was nothing compared to the ten-mile hauling of our first expedition.

While we were moving in supplies, the carpenter and his gang were going ahead with the houses, and the little people of Antarctica, the Adélie penguins, came streaming in to look us over. Three of them toddled into camp and inspected every building nearing completion, almost as if they had been a committee appointed for the purpose. They continued to follow us around until one of them got too close to a dog team. That was the end of that penguin, and the others left us altogether; we never saw them again.

That Sunday, January 28, after a chicken dinner at the base, our first relaxation since the moment we landed, I drove down to the cache to take on a load of dog crates. For the first time, I began to recapture the spirit of Antarctica. Perhaps it was due to the great Emperor penguin that greeted me on the Barrier, nodding his head. He wasn't a bit afraid as I walked up to him—just stood there looking at me as if to say, "You back again, old man?"

When the *Bear* returned from her eastern explorations, I drove down to meet her. They had had a hard time getting out of the pack, but had penetrated further east than any other ship before her and had discovered much new land.

When the few remaining supplies were unloaded from the *Bear,* she slipped her lines from the Bay of Whales. It was the first day of February; she was the last ship we would see until another year had passed. Now a feeling of homesickness came over me that I had never felt before, as three of us, Paul Siple, Dick Moulton, and myself, stood alongside on the ice.

As we waved to the old *Bear* and watched her out of sight, I understood what I had not known before in my eagerness for adventure—I understood what I had seen in other men's faces as silence fell upon us. There is no place on the face of the earth which can produce silence like Antarctica—or more startling noises. I had watched the pressure ice relentlessly pile up day after day at the edge of the Barrier with never-ending cannonlike roars as it broke apart, sounding like the defiance of some monster that refused to die. I had seen men, and been myself, subdued by fear, as we retreated before the turmoil of rifting ice that piled huge blocks on top of one another—heaving, crashing, splitting blocks—expecting a crevasse to open at our feet at any moment. But there are times and places where silence reigns supreme—when on a calm day the eardrums seem to crack with a kind of mental strain that goes with such silence. Then one hears the "roar" of a noiseless atmosphere.

So it was when the last ship pulled out, leaving us marooned in a world of utter desolation. On the first expedition I had given little thought to what was behind me; but now Ada and my little Gloria were back there, nine thousand miles away, where the ship was going; and I thought: When will I see them again?

A great loneliness such as I had never known before swept through me. The inexpressible grandeur and beauty of Antarctica in her best hours was now intensified by the wish that Ada and Gloria could see and share them with me; but the desolation and hazards of her ugliest moods were made worse by the vast distance. It was as if I had been carried away to another planet, away from the earth that held those I loved.

But these are things one cannot talk about. We three, Paul, Dick, and I, turned our faces south; we could not afford to think about the North and our homeland. We had work to do.

3

WITH the long Antarctic night before us, we were now working seven days a week. When the weather was favorable, the
beauty of the great ice Barrier overshadowed its desolation.
You could see West Cape as it stood out into the Ross Sea,
casting the shadow of its icy cliffs far into the Bay of Whales.
Many black spots dotted the bay ice; they were Weddell seals
lying on their backs, sunning themselves, restoring energy and
putting on fat for the cold months ahead when there would be
no sun and they would have only a blowhole to breathe through.
They slept soundly, without fear. For here there was no polar
bear, as in the north, to sneak up and break their necks with
one stroke of a mighty paw.

A skua gull soared overhead, a scavenger watching for anything that looked like food. And there, on the edge of the
Barrier, high above the water, was the Emperor penguin,
monarch of all he surveyed in that great stillness.

Here indeed was beauty, but I was not deceived by it. I
knew how cruel it could be. Within twenty-four hours it turned
colder, and a biting wind burned our faces as we drove our
dogs in from the Barrier cache with our loads of supplies.

I was driving a team of wolf dogs, the largest and strongest of all the dogs. Most of them had been poor-looking specimens after their trip down from Alaska, and some of the drivers thought they were no good, while others were afraid of them — so they became mine. I had long ago learned not to judge dogs hastily. The wolf dog could never surpass the huskies in brains, but they made up for it in strength; and though they required constant attention, I knew they would make a good team if I could find the right Eskimo dog to lead them. What I wouldn't have given if St. Lunaire could have been there! The husky I chose and trained was King, a magnificent specimen of Eskimo dog, much larger and stronger than St. Lunaire had been, though not his equal as a lead dog. King had not been trained to it young enough, and his hearing and sight were not as keen. I had to watch the trail to see that he stayed on it, whereas with St. Lunaire leading I could have closed my eyes and followed.

King was a one-man dog who fortunately liked me and accepted me as his master. He was brown in color, with a white ring around his neck, and ears that stood up like pyramids above his head. He weighed ninety pounds and carried his plumed tail proudly way up over his back. He led his team with royal dignity, as if he knew the meaning of his name. But he always tried to show his joy and affection when I approached him by wagging his tail, letting out a whining noise, and rubbing his head against my leg.

He did have some bad habits. He liked to show his authority, and was very jealous, wanting more than his share of the petting, and resenting any fondness I might show other dogs when he was around. He had a hair-raising howl that used to startle me when I heard him at night, thinking he was out to kill, or that he was being killed; but that was never the case. Sometimes he got sulky and, if he fancied any grievance, did the opposite of what he should do. And how he hated to be aroused in the morning from his warm bed of snow when it came time to harness up! But he always pulled his share of the load with the big wolf dogs who looked to him as their leader. So I was nonetheless grateful to King despite my memories of St. Lunaire; one could not expect to find two dogs like that in a lifetime.

My beautiful little Siberian husky, Gray Cloud, was a good follower, but he was neither big enough nor strong enough even to be considered as a leader for the huge wolf dogs. He was so much smaller than any of my dogs that I had allowed him to be teamed with the smaller dogs of another driver. It was not long, however, before I regretted my decision. It was the first time this driver had ever driven dogs, and he did not have much patience with them. To exact obedience he would always use the whip, while I seldom did this except to break up a fight; and even then I knew just where to hit them, so it would not hurt more than necessary.

When I saw how Gray Cloud was being treated, I offered to trade one of my big dogs for him, which was agreeable to all concerned—especially to Gray Cloud, who did his very best for me in appreciation.

Our work was still hauling in supplies to the base from the Barrier cache. It was good flying weather, with excellent visibility, so the two planes, the Condor and the Beechcraft, were in the air on their mapping flights. The construction work at the base was proceeding slowly. As the house was put together in sections, each section weighing five hundred pounds, it was no little job to get them in place. When the house was nearly finished, some of us moved into it, glad of the warmth. The cracking noise from the big snow-melting tank near the stove kept us awake all the first night. But the bunks were comfortable, wide and long enough to hold our personal belongings at the foot of our sleeping bags.

This main building measured 60 x 24 feet on the inside. It had a main floor and a false floor, with enough space between for the heat to circulate. The bunks were three high, with eighteen tiers ranged on one side and fifteen on the other. In the center were four tables, seating eight at each. At the east end was the galley, with the big cooking stove. At the west was a smaller stove and Dr. Fraiser's hospital. Near the ceiling were hung baskets for drying out wet clothes and boots.

By the tenth of February all hands were moved in, and for the first time we made a full holiday of Sunday, celebrating with a turkey dinner, and talking and resting the rest of the day. But there was a lot of hard work still to be done.

Finally we finished hauling in the food cache from the Barrier; but meanwhile two men had been down in the pressure ice every day killing seals for the dog food during the winter night. So now we started hauling in the seals and putting them in a row near the place where we would build the dog tunnels.

Nearly all our sleds were broken from hauling freight in such big loads, so my next job was lashing and cutting them down to make them lighter for the trip we were planning in March to the Rockefeller Mountains. Three men would winter at a base we were to set up there.

All the supplies would be hauled by dog team, but a tractor tank was going to try to go part way with a 12 x 12 foot house. If it failed, the 500-pound sections of the house would make clumsy loads for a dog sled. We could do it, given time, for I had hauled as much as 2,400 pounds with one team on a hard trail; but 1,100 pounds would be all we would dare try on the 125-mile haul to the mountains. Besides, March was the month of the worst blizzards, and previous experience had proved that no party should be on the trail after the last of March, and preferably no later than the fifteenth.

There is a limit, even for dogs; and though I packed my duffel bag for the trail and set out in a blizzard on the second of March to lay a line of flags east toward the Rockefeller Mountains, I knew it would depend on the tractor whether we could make it now, or whether we would have to wait until the Antarctic night was over. I personally had no faith in tractors. There has never been anything in the Antarctic to equal dog teams for all-around work and dependability. I admit that my prejudice was strengthened by hours of back-breaking labor digging tractors out of crevasses and snowdrifts. I could not help feeling more secure in a blizzard with a team of dogs straining in their harness, and seal blubber and dog-pemmican on the sled for fuel instead of gasoline.

That was why I watched the preparations of the tractor tank with mixed emotions. Our success and perhaps even our safety depended on my being wrong.

4

WHEN the loaded sleds were chained to the tractor and ready to go, the whole camp was on hand to give it a good send-off. Every man in camp owned a camera, and shutters were snapping on all sides of it. The three men, dressed in furs, were getting their pictures taken, as no one knew what the outcome would be for them on the trail. As soon as it was heated up, the engine purred like a huge cat anxious to be under way.

Finally the word was given. The tractor churned and yanked, but could not budge the loaded sleds one inch. A sled was pulled up to give a little slack in the chain, and the tractor got into motion but stopped after ten yards. It backed and yanked, backed and yanked again, to no avail. Men cleared the snow with shovels, but still she held fast. Finally, one sled was detached, and after a lot of grinding and slipping of the caterpillars the tractor moved outside camp and went one hundred yards. There it was stopped again in a drift of snow.

Another sled was unhitched, and on it went again. The men shoveled and heaved, backed and yanked for five miles, but could go no further. Leaving the tractor 120 miles short of their destination, they stumbled back into camp on foot and the journey was given up. I felt no satisfaction in having been right.

Now the whole burden would fall to the dogs, as I had feared.

However, it was decided that it was too late in the season to risk going out on the trail, so the whole idea of establishing a base at the mountains was abandoned. We were disappointed, for we had anticipated the trip for weeks. Now we would have to postpone it until the lowering sun returned. The shortened hours of the long, south-pointing shadows and the dropping temperature were a warning for us to finish digging in for the winter. The darkness waited for no one, and when the blizzards came on we would have to know where everything was, or we would never find it. When one has to dig boxes out of snow-drifts in a blizzard during the black, deep-freezing night, one wishes he had never seen the Antarctic.

The shovel was the most needed and most hated tool of an Antarctic base. Three of us had been digging a tunnel seven feet deep and four feet wide from the "Crystal Palace" (toilet) to the main building. We thought we'd finished when the worst blizzard of the season filled it up again. We hadn't covered it over enough. That was one of the lessons of the Antarctic. Again and again you shoveled a path or a tunnel, and the next day you started in all over again. You learned not to get mad about it. You just laughed and started to dig.

Finally, a day came I had been waiting for; the weather was clear and we took time off to visit the old base at Little America I, six miles away. I hauled three men on my sled and skied ahead of my dogs, urging them on as I could hardly wait to get there. Everyone else was doing the same, the men with teams and the men on skis.

Everyone was feeling good, both men and dogs, though no one could have explained why — perhaps each for a different reason. For once we weren't hauling great loads of supplies but were racing purely for pleasure. For some it was the excitement of a search for buried treasure that drove them on; and for the oldtimers, haunting memories. For me it was something of both.

The sun was out, though low, foretelling its early departure. Soon we would no longer see it until the four-month Antarctic night had passed. With all our hurry, it took us two hours to get to our destination, for we stopped to lay a line of flags so we could find our way back again, if we wanted or needed to, in the dark.

As we topped the hill of ice that led down to Little America I, several of us shouted, "There she is!"

But all we could see was the protruding tops of two lonely radio towers, and seeing this desolate place where I had spent so many months ten years before, I was suddenly overwhelmed by a flood of memories. There was not a sign of any buildings, and only forty-five to fifty feet of the old seventy-foot towers were left sticking up out of the snow.

The snow crunched under the feet of my team as they tore down the hill after me, as if they too sensed the excitement of this moment. We drew up near the towers, but there was no indication even on close inspection of where the houses might be. We each grabbed a shovel and began digging furiously in every direction, stopping only to catch our breaths or to take pictures.

"Here she is!" someone cried; but it was only a skylight.

Finally the cover of a hatch four feet down was uncovered. We prized it up and went down into tunnels sixteen feet below the surface of the snow. Yet this was only the second expedition camp, Little America II, where I had never been. The old tunnel of the first expedition was another ten feet below, and now so small that I had to crawl through it on hands and knees. The hole going into it was no bigger than a barrel, and

I in my fur parka could just slide through it. Then, with head-lights and flashlights, we had to crawl on our hands and knees for a quarter mile to the first base camp.

How many times those years before I had walked this same tunnel with ease! Now in places we could barely squeeze through, wondering all the while if we could get back out again. Suppose it collapsed while we were inside?

In the more open tunnels and buildings of the second camp, Little America II, there was great activity and excited voices. Everyone was ransacking the village buried under the Ant-arctic snows for souvenirs with all the excitement of kids play-ing pirate, and I joined in to find something to take home to Ada. The second expedition had been provided with dishes bearing the pictures of the ships, *City of New York* and the *Bear*, as well as pictures of a dog and an airplane. What would please her more than one of these dishes for her collection? Since she had always wanted a big platter, I made this my project.

We couldn't get into the main tunnel which led to the old Mess Hall; but wherever a man could go, we went. Our hands were filled with plunder, but I wasn't satisfied. I had not found a platter for Ada.

Well, I would go back sometime and look again; but I little thought just then that this simple objective would sustain my hope through the longest, loneliest Antarctic night of my expe-rience, and that I would set out in a blizzard in the dark night to fulfill it.

When we returned to base, we settled into a routine once again. It was getting colder and colder, the days shorter and shorter; and darkness was fast coming upon us. We started work on the dog tunnels that should have been done long before. No matter how our backs ached, we had to keep going so the dogs would be protected. A dog might dig down in the snow and survive a few days, but when the temperature goes to 70° below zero, no flesh can endure it without shelter. Your breath freezes as it comes out of your mouth, and you hear a ruffling sound like the wings of a small bird flying close to your ears. There is a miniature thunderstorm in your lungs, and men spit blood if they work too hard or move around too fast. The moisture of your body condenses in your clothes and freezes there. You will feel all right while you are working, but beware when you stop and the circulation of the blood slows down. Body heat must be kept built up. Men working at low temperatures in the polar regions often do not realize this, until it may be too late.

Figuring a cubic foot of hard-packed snow as weighing 25 pounds, we had to move more than 2.5 million pounds of it. My tunnel was finished and the dogs under shelter just before another blizzard came in on a forty- to fifty-mile wind. The dogs still outside took a terrible beating, and somehow we had to get them protected, even though their tunnels were not ready.

The air was so thick with snow that we could not see our hands before us. Hanging onto thirty feet of alpine rope to keep from being separated, four of us ventured out into the storm. It took us some time to dig out the dogs even after we had found them. By leading in nine dogs at a time, all seven teams were eventually under shelter. We had dogs all over our own quarters, since tunnels were ready for only two teams. But no one objected to it and the dogs promptly lay down and went to sleep, grateful for the warmth.

I could not help but marvel at their spirit, which even the toughest weather does not break. They can be whining and crying in agony, sheltering their heads with their bodies, their hair one mat of ice and snow; but let their master appear with a harness, and they will respond with excitement and friendliness.

They will frolic and roll in the icy snow, taking off with the sled at a full gallop, loving the feeling of going somewhere again.

Such is the unpredictable nature of Antarctic weather that in a few hours the blizzard had cleared, and everything looked so peaceful and beautiful that it seemed incredible it had been so rough so short a time before. It often worked the other way, too. Out of a clear sky a little puff of wind would come, in five minutes it would be snowing hard, and in an hour, a blizzard would be raging.

The lower the sun sank, the more beautiful the sunsets became. Often the entire sky to the north was illuminated. Sometimes there were large black clouds with many-colored lights streaming through. Then a gorgeous red flame would cast long shadows, painting the tips of every ridge and pinnacle of ice. Great streamers would cross the sky from north to south, drawing colors from clouds or by reflection from the ice and snow.

On the twenty-first of April, the Stars and Stripes flew for the last time, and the sun was officially considered to be "gone." The whole camp fell in line south of the flagpole for the ceremony of pulling down the flag at noon. As two marines lowered it, every man took off his cap for a split second—which was as long as we dared leave our heads uncovered. Slowly our flag was drawn down, folded up, and put away until the sun would make its appearance four months hence. The Antarctic Night had begun.

5

THERE was still a cheery spot of glow on the northern horizon to mark off the brief days, but its duration became less and less as total darkness engulfed Antarctica. The Bay of Whales froze over, and the seals stayed underneath the ice. The penguins left for their winter rookeries. The skua gull, too, flew north to a warmer climate. We were left alone. For a while our days would be a milky mist; then one day would stretch into the next and then the next without any change from darkness to light.

Now the monotony begins to prey on nerves. We go about our work almost in a daze, stumbling and tripping over things in the deceiving diffusion of dim light that marks off the Antarctic autumn day.

We get up in what we call the "morning." The night watchman throws open the door as he makes his morning round to build the fires in the stoves and to call the cook and the messman. I can hear him as he tiptoes across the floor. His fur mukluks sound like a rat scampering. Then I hear the rattle of dishes as the messman sets the table for breakfast, and the noise from the galley as the cook puts coal in the stove, creating fumes of smoke which drift from one end of the room to the other.

The mess cook calls once, but no one moves. Then he goes around and shakes each man separately, saying the same thing every time, "Get up and grab it." Unconsciously we develop a routine. The bunks are in three tiers, and first one man rolls out, then another and then the other—always in the same order. How slowly I roll out of my sleeping bag, hurrying only when I hit the cold floor. The house is not warm yet, and while I lose no time getting into my clothes, I think how nice it would be to get back into the sleeping bag.

After breakfast I start dressing for outdoors, wondering to myself: What shall I put on today?

Automatically I ask, "How cold is it this morning?"

"Fifty below, and going down."

That means it's necessary to dress warmly for outdoor work. Without the proper clothing it doesn't take long to freeze face, hands, or feet. So I think, I must put on my fur mukluks and my reindeer fur mitts, for the wind cuts like a knife and the handle of a shovel is like a red-hot iron.

Then I wander around, start a conversation with someone, or end up at the now glowing stove, waiting for something to happen.

Someone calls the snow-melting gang to work, men whose turn comes around every two weeks. Two men grab the saws, and as they cut out blocks of snow, another man with a shovel breaks them free. Three other men carry them about fifty yards to the roof of the house, now snowed under, and put them down a chute to the tank.

When enough has been put in, a man from the galley yells, "She is full!" and the whole gang runs for the house where the hot stove awaits them.

The rest of the day each goes about his daily routine of work, building the Blubber House, perhaps, or hauling seals in and giving the dogs their daily meal. The meat has to be cut from seal that is frozen at 60° to 70° below zero. We have to keep our wits about us, or the ax handle will break. Nowhere else in the world does wood get so brittle. A little twist of the handle, or cutting a bone on a slant, will break or splinter it.

The seals were laid in long rows over which the wind had piled about four feet of snow. It was no easy matter to get out enough meat for all the dogs every day and soon it would be worth our lives even to try it, so we started working on a tunnel, four feet wide and long enough to store 150 seals. We would start work in the little spell of twilight that marked off the days, though it was even hard to see and dig in that milky light. When it became completely dark, we either had to quit or get our lanterns going. Usually then a wind would spring up and the snow would drift in almost as fast as we could throw it out.

When the tunnel was finished and the weather sufficiently clear, we started the major task of hauling in the seals, some of them weighing as much as six hundred pounds. With a block and tackle, and after much hard pulling and straining, we succeeded in getting several inside. It took a crew of four men — two outside to hook the seals onto the tackle and steer them to the end of the tunnel, and two inside to pull them in and stack them in place. They were, of course, frozen solid and very awkward to handle. Fortunately, the driver of the tractor came to our assistance, and I was quick to pay tribute to the very real worth of a tractor at home base. Even with this help we all had lame backs, but with the tractor doing the pulling, all 150 seals were stored away in fairly quick time.

Then the dog tunnels had to be completed. We had to be sure that no dog could get loose, for if one did a fight was almost certain. And if someone was not right there to break it up, it would be only a matter of minutes before one of them would be torn to pieces.

The plan for the dog tunnels was to have five on one side and four on the other, at right angles to a main tunnel. Thus each team would have its own quarters. We dug the tunnels like deep trenches in the snow, covering the top first with boards laid crosswise, then putting on a layer of chicken wire, and finally canvas. Blocks of snow were put all along the sides and covered over with loose snow to fill all cracks and keep the snow from drifting in.

In each tunnel the dogs were chained separately. Holes were dug in the sides, a sufficient distance apart to set the crates in. Then a piece of 2" x 4" wood was driven down deep into the snow near the end of the crate and the dog chain was bound around both this stake and the crate itself and attached to the dog's choke collar. The harder he pulled, the tighter the collar became, and the dogs soon learned respect for it. Skis, ski poles, and sleds were all hung from the roof of the tunnel to prevent the dogs from chewing on them.

Besides these jobs, there were the planes to dig in and cover over, although it was now 40° below zero and extremely difficult to work out of doors. We cut huge blocks of snow and passed them up to a man who used them to build a sheltering wall, fifteen feet high. Although we were plenty stiff at night from this routine, strangely enough, because of the temperature, we were not as tired as we would have been under similar circumstances back home.

Whenever I could, in the last diffusion of light which remained to us, I took Gray Cloud for a walk. To his great delight I let him race over the Barrier and we both found pleasure in our outings. I would also let him lie in my bunk until he began to get too warm and it was time to return him to the tunnel, where I dared not show him any special attention for fear of arousing the jealousy of King. Poor little Gray Cloud would have been no match for any of the other dogs on the team.

When the work was done, Dick Moulton and I would go down to the Blubber House and listen to the fire roar as we talked. The Blubber House was really nothing but a hole in the snow, covered over with canvas supported by bamboo poles. We used it for cutting up seal meat and melting the fat down to make dog pemmican for use on the trail in the spring. We reached it through a tunnel leading off from the network of dog tunnels, and it provided a retreat where we felt almost as if we were living in another world where it was a very special and peculiar pleasure simply to be able to talk, about anything at all. Our minds felt strangely relieved.

We might start talking of something in the present, how we could never have moved in the seals without the tractor, for instance; but soon we would be talking about home and the past. That off our minds, we would switch to the future, talking about the big trip we were planning to make when the sun returned, and about the special dog pemmican we were going to make up for it. The round-trip would be more than 1,200 miles, and we might take as long as three months for it. We were going beyond the Rockefeller Mountains to Hal Flood Mountain, to build a cairn and plant the Stars and Stripes. It was the big goal that made the prospect of the long, dark night endurable for me, but it was a long way off, and I lured myself on from day to day with the growing prospect of my private project: to go back to Little America I and II and dig down again to find a platter for Ada.

One day Dick and I decided we wanted two wooden barrels to make a bathtub for our blubber house. They had been unloaded from the *Bear* at the Barrier cache, and at the first opportunity we drove down, racing over the Barrier with Dick's team of little Siberians.

The days were now marked solely by a brief and eerie twilight in which dawn was quickly swallowed by night. Driving through the milky wave, the annual remnant of the Antarctic day, we could not tell whether we were going uphill or down, except from the speed the dogs were making.

Of what little could be seen, everything looked alike. A haycock of ice that you could hang your hat on looked the same as a mountain miles away. We saw something black ahead of us that looked like seals out in the bay, but almost immediately we were right on top of them—the edges of barrel heads sticking up out of the snow—the very barrels we had come for.

From where we stood, when we looked out over the Bay of Whales toward West Cape, the edge of the Barrier appeared to be on a straight line and level with the bay ice. The Barrier itself had disappeared.

We seemed to be only a few feet from the edge, so we started out very slowly and cautiously to investigate, not knowing when we might walk off the edge of the ice shelf, if it was still there. Nothing happened. We kept on walking. At last, a few feet away, we could see where the Barrier actually fell off, with a perpendicular drop of a hundred feet or more.

We stopped and looked out into space, thinking of what a contrast this was to the days when we had gazed on the same scene with the bay as bright as a mirror, reflecting the rays of the sun. Now all its glamour was shrouded in darkness, and the Barrier was truly the lost continent. We found ourselves speaking in whispers as one instinctively does in all quiet places where there is an indefinable spirit that awes the soul. Facing the northern dawn of dim light from a sun that no longer rose above the horizon, the stillness laid its chill hand upon us and spoke not of the beauty that had been, but of some great calamity that had befallen this land of darkness—and it was as if we were the only two who had survived it and we dared not look back.

Suddenly we couldn't take it any more; so we wheeled on our skis, shivering as we made our way back, jumping from one wavelike snow ridge or "sastrugi" to another, and dodging ghostlike pinnacles of ice that seemed to be moving toward us out of the night, coming to life, blocking our way.

6

WE loaded the barrels on the sled and released the dogs for a race against the darkness. Until we tipped the rise on the Barrier we could see hardly anything; then the light on the mast of the antenna pole beckoned us to warmth and food and shelter.

You cannot possibly appreciate what cheery brightness even a dim light can put into one's heart until you have come upon one yourself to guide you out of a wilderness. But once we had tasted the peace of the Barrier's stillness, we came to dread the turmoil of too much "society." It was as if we had been initiated into something that set us apart from those who had not shared it. We wanted to keep that "something" alive for ourselves.

Dick and I worked hard on our Blubber House, making it as cosy as possible. As well as making our dog pemmican there, we planned to make it a retreat where we could study and escape all the noise of the Mess Hall, where it was almost impossible to concentrate. The Scientific House was just as bad, with the radio always going and the scientists all working and talking back and forth to one another. There was not a man on the expedition whom we did not like; but the noise was very confusing to one coming in from that great stillness. There were only four or five of us to work out of doors, and we worked so hard that we longed for a little rest and peace. So Dick and I planned to get away by ourselves for a while. When the work eased up we would sledge in the dark to the site of the old bases and camp there a few days. This would give me a chance to dig down once more in search for the big platter I wanted to take home to Ada.

Dick was as eager as I to make the trip to Little America I. We didn't tell anyone about our plans for fear it would be objected to as an unnecessary risk, which of course it was. But it gave us something to talk about and kept us from getting restless.

We kept putting it off, for one reason or another. First we thought we would wait to see if the weather would warm up a little. It was 60° below zero and going down. Before the week was out the temperature was down almost to a record—71° below—although we had beat that on the first expedition with 72.2° below zero.

Our flashlights would freeze, and so would the kerosene in our lanterns, putting out the lights. When we were in the tunnels feeding the dogs and this happened, it was a serious predicament if we were among dogs who did not know us. The possibility of having a leg torn by a snap of their powerful jaws was very real. For however friendly someone else's dogs might be under normal conditions, the Eskimo dog is very nervous and highly excitable upon very little provocation. For instance, he is gun-shy, and the report of a shot will make him coil up. The snow settling as he walks over it will cause him to jump and pull out to one side. A quick motion of the hand will make him stop in his tracks. He is quick to notice things out of the ordinary, and very seldom forgets. He will fight another dog for no reason at all, and already seven of our dogs had been killed in this way.

You must understand this, and know how to talk to them boldly but kindly, to reassure them and to keep up your own courage until you work your way to an entrance, or to one of your own dogs.

Chips, our carpenter, went out into the dog tunnel one day to fix a crate. The dogs were continually chewing on them, probably out of boredom. They resented being idle, and being chained in one place all the time was a severe test of their patience. Chips put his lantern down near the spot where he was going to work. A stray puppy that was running up and down the tunnel snatched the lantern and made away with it, leaving Chips there in the dark with a pack of dogs that scarcely knew him, or he them.

He was in real fear for his life. No one would ever hear him call, and it would be a long and cold wait until one of the dog men came to feed the dogs. A full-blooded wolf lay near the entrance of the tunnel he had to pass. Fortunately, out of the hundred dogs he knew one within his reach he could trust. Holding him by the collar on the side toward the wolf, and with a hammer in the other hand and his muscles ready to use it, he got by.

When we saw him coming in through the door leading a dog, we all started to razz him, asking him since when he had become so fond of dogs.

He told us, "This dog has just saved my life," and demanded a leg of mutton for him from the cook.

So then we put electric lights in the tunnels. This did not make it any warmer, but it was more pleasant for both men and dogs. I felt sorry for the men who did not have this companionship and diversion. In the lighted tunnels there were always friends to greet me, wagging their tails, jumping the full length of their chains and nuzzling my leg with their noses. I would talk to each one as I gave them their hunks of seal meat, patting them on the head or cuffing their ears with affection.

One morning I found the tail of one of my dogs so frozen in the ice I had to pull it loose for him. He had lain down outside of his crate and couldn't get up again. After that, I put straw in my tunnel for the dogs to lie on and they acted like a bunch of overgrown puppies about it. King tossed it around, tore it apart, and had the time of his life. So did I, watching them go in and out of their crates, making their beds. After they had the straw nicely arranged, they would sniff it and start pulling it out again.

One of my wolf dogs was called Mopey, because he had slit eyes and always looked sleepy. When I first saw him, he was a very sorry-looking fellow and he wouldn't let anyone go near him. But sleepy as he looked, he always pulled his share with the rest of them.

Then there was Bo, who had seemed to be a cripple, so I had left him on the tethering line to which the dogs were chained when not in harness. Two or three days later, he seemed to be so well that I was able to hitch him up.

Tim looked like a big timber wolf, and had a bit of the sneak about him. When I fed the dogs seal meat, I generally gave them half blubber and half meat. If I gave him his blubber first, Tim would not eat it, but would bark until I had given him his piece of meat.

Moody was black with two marks over his eyes that made him look as if he had four eyes. Actually, he had only one. He was an old veteran of another expedition, and knowing him as I did, I knew that a driver could never have been justified in hitting him with a whip. But that is what had put out his eye. I was willing to bet that Moody knew more than that driver, for he was my wheel dog (which means the rear dog on the team, nearest the sled), and I never had to tell him what to do. He was gentle as a lamb, always had a friendly greeting for his master, and there was no better-behaved dog in Antarctica. He was always on the job, minding his own business and doing his share of the work, asking nothing in return but a little food, and a pat on the head now and then—and a look of affection that seemed to mean a great deal to him.

I had another big fellow that I called Duke, who carried his ears and nose high as if proud of his name. He had some wolf in him, but I would swear that the rest was St. Bernard. Every time I went by him he would take hold of my hand in a friendly way, as if to say, "What is your hurry, old man? Have you got nothing for me this time?"

Down near the lower end of the tunnel, next to King, was a mischievous dog named Pat, who was the laziest of all. He was such a great big fellow that he ought to have been ashamed of himself for the way he tried to make me believe he was working hard when all the time he was only bluffing.

At the head of the tunnel was the little beauty of them all, Gray Cloud. He knew he belonged to me more than any of the rest. Every morning his face would beam when he saw me, and he would sit proudly up on his haunches, holding out a paw in greeting. But I never let the other dogs see me favoring him with choice tidbits. That was our secret. I was proud of him because he always did his best to pull his share in harness, though he had never been trained for it. And in my lonely hours, so far from home, he was the tangible embodiment of all the love which had made him a part of my family. He had absorbed their love and now, with both of us buried beneath the snow at the bottom of the world, he was giving it back to me when I needed it.

When most of the work was squared away, Dick and I

finally got permission to go to Little America when the weather moderated. Ours was to be an official mission to bring back radio tubes, light bulbs, and tracing paper. We had orders to hold a radio schedule with the base, and return in thirty-six hours if we could not keep in contact. So the radio was important, and I spent a great deal of time practicing with it.

Our tent had to be dried out and trail-marking flags made ready. We had to pack fuel for our primus stove, check over our sleeping bags and fur clothing, and make up enough dog food for nine dogs. In attending to these tasks, we escaped the monotony which plagued the other men who were not engaged in scientific projects.

The Scientific House was a busy place those days, with all of the scientists hard at work on their individual projects. There was Dr. Lockhart with his chemistry; and next to him, Arnold Court, the meteorologist. On the other side was the desk of Murray Wiener, the night watchman and aurora observer. Then came Jack Perkins, the biologist; geologists Charlie Passel and Larry Warner; Harold Gilmore, the recorder; and Dr. Wade, the senior scientist.

The photographer, Charlie Shirley, had a nice little dark room of his own where I used to help him print pictures. Leonard Berlin, the surveyor, and Raymond Butler, the cartographer, had their own room too, where they made maps. Leonard was to go with Dick and myself on the long trip in the spring, to survey the mountains for mapping.

Finally the great day came. The weather cleared and though there was no sun to warm the air, the temperature came up to 26° below zero. We took our sled out of the tunnel and lashed tanks on it to hold our supplies.

When everything was loaded and ready, we took the chains off Dick's team of little Siberians and let them race out of the tunnel. They were so excited to be able to stretch their legs and race around in the snow that it required a great deal of coaxing and calling before we finally got them all in harness. Finally we put on our skis and at last were off into the black night.

We had not gone half a mile before it started to snow again, blacking out the tower light and all the camp beneath it. We had miners' lights fastened to our foreheads as we maneuvered back and forth to find the flags with which we had earlier marked the trail. When we found them, we stopped to set our course for Little America.

7

ONLY those who have driven dogs in the Arctic or Antarctic can realize how hard it is to keep a straight course with only a compass for guidance, when mist or snow obscures the sun or stars. The compass first swung one way and then the other; sometimes the needle made a complete circle. With the rocking of the sled as it went over the snow ridges or sastrugi, and the veering of the dogs in the dark, we had our hands full, particularly as the blinding snow shut off the beams of our flashlights. The trip was not nearly as much pleasure as we had expected.

The fact that our goal was only six miles away is all that justified our continuing, and even that is open to question. When the sled meter trailing behind us showed we had gone seven miles, we stopped. If we had been drifting west, that distance would have taken us over the edge of the Barrier and into the Bay of Whales.

We could not be far from our destination; and rather than take any more chances, we decided to camp right where we were. There was a bad crevasse area just a short distance from Little America, and we feared getting into it through an erratic compass, tired dogs, and blinded eyes.

By the time our tent was up the wind had died down and

the snow had stopped. I tried calling the base, and finally heard them, but could not make them hear me. So we crawled into our bags for the night.

That was the coldest night I have ever spent. And when we crawled out, the moon was up and shining through clouds on fog that had settled down like a blanket over the whole Barrier. We could not see a thing.

Again I tried to contact West Base, but without success, and finally we gave up and got into our sleeping bags again. I was so cold that I lay for four hours without sleeping. The next time I stuck my head through the hole in the tent, I saw beautiful clear moonlight, with visibility clear to the pressure ice down in the Bay of Whales. So I called to Dick that we had better get going while we could. There was a black mist to the north, and it might cloud up again any moment.

Once under way, with the moon ahead of us, it was blind traveling, and soon the mist closed in and blotted out the moon. The dogs were whining because it was so cold; but there was no wind and they were anxious to keep going. The snow was scrunching beneath the runners like sand, and we began to feel uneasy, traveling now by instinct alone and not seeming to get anywhere. So we veered almost a half circle and started off again.

We were headed north when I looked to the west and could just distinguish the old radio towers that marked Little America. Our destination reached, we succeeded at last in contacting the base and informing them we had arrived safely. With everyone relieved, we settled down for some sleep before digging.

When we woke, Dick started digging down to the Scientific House, and I went to work where I thought the radio shack ought to be. We shoveled fast to keep warm, and finally scraped the cover of a hatch. Sixteen feet below was the second-expedition tunnel, and ten feet lower, the small hole to the oldest tunnel.

With headlights and flashlights, we crawled what seemed an endless way to Little America I. At last we reached the coal bunker, where we had to go through head first, like seals sliding down a blowhole.

The old Norwegian House where I had slept for one long year now held no charms for me. The walls were ready to cave in, the bunks were smashed to pieces, and everything was covered with grime and littered with dirt. There was something so desolate and forbidding about it that it made one hesitate to trespass. If anyone had told me ten years before that I would come back in the dark and crawl down through two buried camps to do this thing, I would not have believed him. Without difficulty, we found light bulbs, tracing paper, and folding chairs, which on hands and knees we pushed ahead of us down the dark, damp, narrow tunnel that would soon be closed up altogether, yet I wasn't satisfied. After the weeks of planning and all the trouble, I was determined to find a platter for Ada.

We decided to take a last look around, finally finding a second-expedition tunnel that had not been invaded by any previous salvage party. Dick slid into it first and we were groping our way forward, when he suddenly let out a yell. In my haste, I almost fell over a platter, and as he had found three he gave me one of his, so we should each have two. I could not have been more pleased if we had discovered the South Pole.

But that completely ended the attraction of Little America I and II for both of us. Our intention of camping there for awhile was abandoned and we hurried back to West Base as fast as the dogs could travel.

Glad as we were to get back, there was a difference in the atmosphere which I now felt more keenly because of our trip

TOP: *City of New York* tied up to the ice in the Bay of Whales after a stormy passage. Fresh whale meat hangs in the rigging.

BOTTOM: *City of New York* ready to unload on the bay ice with the Ross Ice Barrier in the distance. (*The National Archives*)

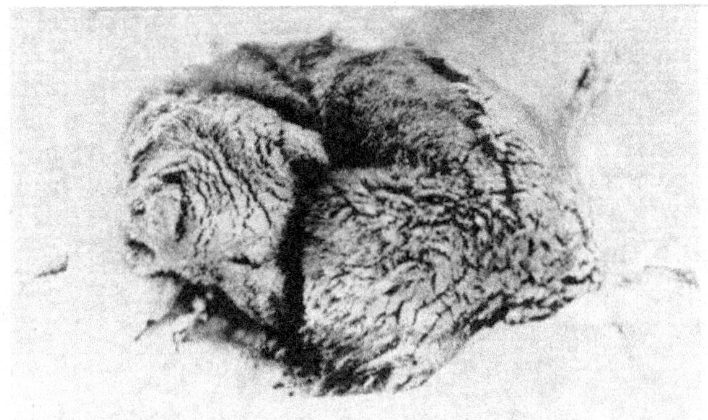

LEFT TOP: Dog teams loaded with equipment and supplies ready to start inland from the *City of New York*. (*The National Archives*)

LEFT BOTTOM: Dogs and men haul the lifeboat up the slope from the bay ice to Little America. (*The National Archives*)

RIGHT TOP: An Eskimo dog sleeping snugly in the snow after the day's work is done.

RIGHT BOTTOM: View of Little America I taken during the long Antarctic night. (*The National Archives*)

LEFT TOP: Scene in the hut at Little America I.

LEFT CENTER: Raising Old Glory for the first time after the end of the winter night and the return of the sun at Little America.

LEFT BOTTOM: Jack Bursey driving his team of huskies with St. Lunaire leading through the pressure ice in the Bay of Whales.

RIGHT TOP: *The Trap*—The crevasse area 150 miles south of Little America gave Bursey and his companions trouble just as it had Amundsen years before on his way to the South Pole. (*The National Archives*)

RIGHT BOTTOM: Bursey at his nearest to the pole, 200 miles from Little America. A snow beacon with flag on top marks the supply cache.

LEFT TOP: A dog team pulling a heavily loaded sled away from a temporary supply dump. The two ships of the expedition, the U.S.S. *Bear* and the U.S.S. *North Star,* are moored to the bay ice. (*Wide World Photos*)
LEFT CENTER AND BOTTOM: Before and after a blizzard at Little America III. (*Wide World Photos*)
RIGHT BOTTOM: Dogs in their winter quarters in the dog-town tunnel. (*The National Archives*)

LEFT TOP: Sunset over the Ross Ice Barrier in 1940. The big snow cruiser can be seen in the distance.

LEFT BOTTOM: One of the sleeping cubicles at Little America III, with Berlin and Bursey in their bunks. (*The National Archives*)

RIGHT TOP: Preparing trail flags for the sledging trips to come. Bursey in the foreground. (*The National Archives*)

RIGHT BOTTOM: Bursey lashing a sled in preparation for spring operations. (*The National Archives*)

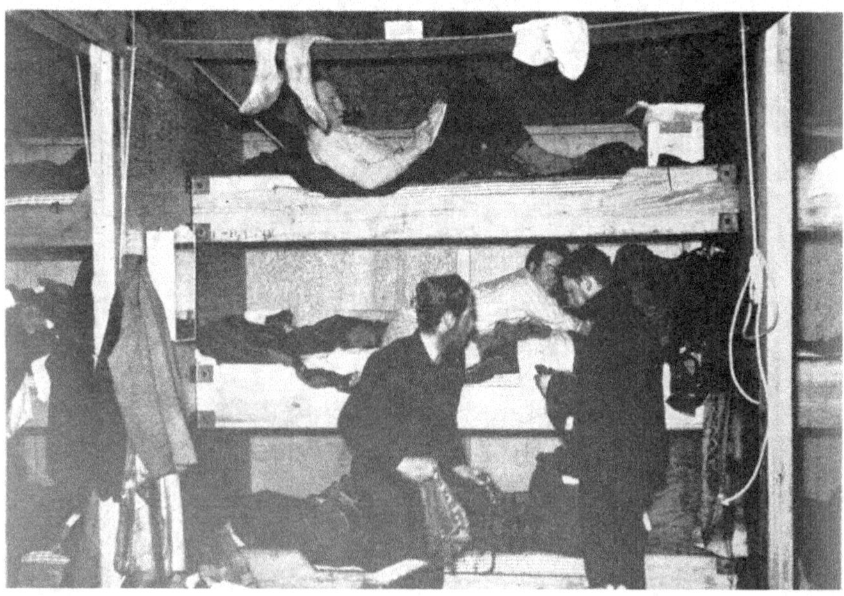

LEFT TOP: July 4 is celebrated with a movie during the long Antarctic night. Bursey second from right in foreground. (*The National Archives*)

LEFT BOTTOM: Dawn in the north of returning sun as seen from the West Base entrance to Little America III. (*The National Archives*)

RIGHT TOP: Bursey and Berlin with Bursey's team led by King ready for the 1220-mile trek that took them and Moulton to an unknown area. (*The National Archives*)

RIGHT BOTTOM: Bursey and his team shortly before taking off on the trip to Hal Flood Mountain. Shown on the right is a meter wheel which is attached to the rear of a sled to measure trail mileage. (*The National Archives*)

LEFT TOP: Berlin, Bursey, and Moulton at Mount Rea on their way to Hal Flood Mountain. (*The National Archives*)

LEFT BOTTOM: Bursey and King, one of the great lead dogs of Antarctic exploration. (*The National Archives*)

RIGHT TOP: The U.S.S. *Bear* upon arrival at the Bay of Whales to evacuate the wintering-over party. (*The National Archives*)

RIGHT BOTTOM: The first meal of the trail parties after their return to Little America. (*The National Archives*)

Admiral Byrd with Jack Bursey raising the Stars and Stripes on the site of Little America I where both had been present at the first raising of the American flag twenty-seven years earlier. In the background is a steel radio tower. Seventy-five feet tall, all but about ten feet of the tower have been covered by snow and ice over the years. (*Wide World Photo*)

LEFT TOP: The East Barrier rising 75 to 200 feet above Kainan Bay.

LEFT CENTER: The mighty icebreaker U.S.S. *Glacier* carving a way through the ice in Kainan Bay on Operation Deepfreeze. (*Wide World Photo*)

LEFT BOTTOM: The U.S.S. *Atka* pushing a berg away from the unloading area at Kainan Bay. (*Wide World Photo*)

RIGHT CENTER: Little America V soon to be covered by deep snow. (*Wide World Photo*)

RIGHT BOTTOM: Bursey's mechanized trail-blazing party leaves Little America V to probe deep into the wastes of Marie Byrd Land preparatory to establishing Byrd Station 600 miles away. (*Wide World Photo*)

TOP: Lt. Cdr. Jack Bursey on the trail during Operation Deepfreeze I.

BOTTOM: Inside a forty-foot crevasse near Little America V. (*Wide World Photo*)

alone in the Antarctic night. Something indefinable seemed to be clouding the minds of some of the men and began to spread over the whole base.

The first tangible thing I noticed was in the behavior of one of the new dog drivers. Instead of cutting off just enough seal meat for one meal for his dogs, he would cut up a whole seal and carry it off, making one trip after another, until it was all hidden away somewhere, leaving the other dog men without any. He would start digging a hole in the snow, and keep on digging, forgetting that it was time for him to stop, or that he was down far enough. There seemed to be something preying on his mind which made him lose all sense of time or environment.

At last, one day, he said he was tired of living, that he was just waiting for a bad enough night, with a strong enough wind, to "take a little walk." No one kidded him about it, but no one really believed it, either.

Now the inky blackness was firmly settled around us, except on rare occasions when the sky was clear and a low moon cast its pale rays south to meet the streamers of the "southern lights."

At first the aurora australis was a novelty, and men ran out of doors to marvel at the sight of the weaving, waving colors that filled the sky. But curiosity was soon cooled by the temperature. It was 60° below again and going down, and the warmth of the hot stove was more attractive. Most of the time the sky was overcast, and we saw this one beautiful phase of the Antarctic night in all its brilliance only a few times on this expedition.

"Morning" came now without distinction from night. No milky twilight marked the day; and when we looked out, or ventured out for necessary work or exercise, we saw only our own light which was kept always burning on the radio tower as a beacon for those who might chance to stray away from camp.

There were always some of us who whenever possible would go skiing for exercise, although it was indescribably lonely, pushing one foot in front of the other, watching the trail flags go by. It was essential to keep the flags in sight, for fear of missing the camp. As I skied along I would think of all the terrible things that might happen—a crevasse unexpectedly opening up, a sudden blizzard obscuring the trail.

Indoors, too, the peculiar spell of the Antarctic night was beginning to take hold of me—I was losing my perspective. Memories would flash through my mind with lightning speed—everything I had ever done or thought of doing, people I had met, incidents in my childhood. As I thought about civilization, home, my loved ones, I would sink into the depression brought on by loneliness.

I had not experienced this feeling on my first expedition. Then the thrill of adventure had sustained me. It took all my will power to snap out of it, to get up and move around instead of sitting in a corner for hours, not speaking to anyone, listening to the dreary noise of the wind rattling the ventilators. I noticed that the men around me were saying very little either. Their thoughts, too, seemed far away.

One night a cold draft was coming from the door and snow was drifting in, but when I tried to close it tight, I could not. The sill was covered with ice where the warm and cold air met. I felt sorry for the man who had the chores to do in the morning—he would have a lot of shoveling. I started for the coalbin for a bucket of coal, but when I put down the bucket to pick up a shovel, to my astonishment I saw that my bucket was a chair. How could I have done that? Then I began to remember how it was on the first expedition when men did similar inexplicable things. Like the time Charlie Gould was chopping ice from the door sill and had placed a lantern nearby. Suddenly he started hollering, "Who's got my lantern? Whoever has it better bring it right back." The lantern was still there where he'd put it. I hadn't understood, then.

Once in my bunk and warm in my reindeer sleeping bag, I felt better. But only for a few minutes. Then my thoughts began to stray again. The distance from home and family seemed insurmountable. I saw no escape. I tried to turn over but felt weighted down by the very tightness of my sleeping bag. It was almost as if someone were sitting on me. No matter how much I wanted to break away from what was building up in my mind, I could not. The bag in which I had slept so peacefully became a trap for thoughts I could not govern.

Lying back in a cold sweat, I tried to relax and succeeded in sleeping a little. But suddenly I was awakened by a jar or series of jolts, a sound like distant thunder—a long, rumbling noise. The Barrier had broken again; another piece had split off into one more northbound iceberg. How far away was it? And how big? It sounded tremendous—millions of tons of ice launched in the sea to menace ships. My thoughts jumped to the *Titanic* and then back to the terrifying thought that perhaps we were on the berg, perhaps the Barrier had broken off behind us. Maybe the whole camp was at this moment on its way to sea, the gap getting larger and larger. Sleep was impossible. I threw back the hood from my sleeping bag and drew in the fresh cold air, which seemed to clear my mind. The moisture of my breath froze as it came out of my mouth, and I studied the curling rings of vapor as they dissolved in the colder air.

8

ONE "day" (we called it that when the house was warm and the prospect of food was before us) a thing happened we never would have believed.

A man walked out into the Antarctic night and disappeared. It was the same man who had said he was only waiting for the right kind of a night to "take a walk."

No one had seen him go. No one had seen him for at least six hours. No sign of him could be found. A sharp wind was blowing, the air was full of snow, and the temperature was about 40° below zero.

Men stared at each other in amazement. They spoke in whispers, leaning up against their bunks, trying to remember, trying to figure it out. One man went to search the dog kennels, but returned and threw his cap down on his berth without saying a word.

Hardly anyone moved, as if fearing to admit what they did not want to believe. Gloom swept through the camp like a cloud of dust. Only one man missing, but suddenly the camp was empty.

Then just as suddenly the spell was broken. The camp came to life. Everyone began putting on his warmest clothing, testing flashlights and lanterns, getting flares ready. Now the silence was broken by a buzz of conversation as search parties were formed. They would go out into the night at the risk of their own lives, to try to save his.

It was a doubtful and hazardous job, with 360 degrees of direction to walk in, and every trail obliterated instantly in the drifting snow. If anyone fell, he would be soon buried and invisible, for in the raging storm no one could see as far as the next man.

It could be seen in every man's face that he believed the search would be useless, but that it was unthinkable not to try. Not one man showed any unwillingness to be included in the search parties.

But first every hole, every corner, every conceivable space in that little community beneath the snow was searched; the outhouse, chopping house, tunnels, supply cache, barrels, boxes— everything that could hide a man.

There was not one trace. The missing man had left no sign, no note of instructions or declaration of intentions.

We all assembled in the mess room and organized ourselves into four groups for an outside search. First we looked for footprints or any other clue that might start us off in the right direction but there was nothing.

So one party went south, one north, one east, and one west— groping our way into the night, stumbling over ridges and crisscrossed sastrugi, yelling at the tops of our voices until we almost gagged from wind and snow down our throats.

In the vast space our little lights were reduced to the proportion of fireflies as we searched the snow for footprints that were not to be seen. And behind us our own tracks were obliterated as fast as we made them; our only clue to direction was the wind, which might change suddenly and leave us without any guide to retrace our steps in the inky blackness.

Suddenly we all felt a compulsion to return. Each man responded to it instantly and independently. We were like men being led by some unseen hand as we plodded our weary way back to shelter with heavy hearts and low spirits because this would be the first real catastrophe of the expedition.

As each party returned, the rest would all look up expectantly, but no one asked the question uppermost in all our minds. No trace whatever of the missing man had been found. The search parties had made a complete circle of the camp, showing lights, shooting up flares and shouting; but not a sound was heard in answer.

Fatigue and strain were written in every face. I had never seen such unanimous and utter defeat in a group of men before. For we were all helpless. There was not one thing we could do in that cold darkness of the Antarctic night.

The fury of the storm increased to a gale, and during the next twenty-four hours it seemed to us as if all the demons in hell were let loose. The guy wires that held the stovepipe and the antenna wires of the radio towers moaned a mournful complaint and warning. Sudden gusts of wind picked up huge blocks of snow and hurled them away into the night. Not one of us could forget that there was a man out there, dead or dying or fighting for his life. There was no conversation about it. If anyone spoke, it was in a depressed whisper as if afraid to disturb someone else's thoughts.

Few slept. Men walked the camp, clinging to hope that dwindled at last, and the missing man's sleeping bag was removed from his berth. His personal effects were examined to find out if possible the nature of his trouble, and some logical explanation for his sudden disappearance.

I strained my mind trying to visualize what had become of

him. If he had gone down wind, he might have walked over the edge of the Barrier and fallen into the Bay of Whales. Or he might have stumbled into any of the many bottomless crevasses. And if he encountered none of these hazards, then he would surely by this time be frozen to death. We might possibly find him when the sun returned; but even that was doubtful because he would certainly by then be well covered with snow.

Sunday morning the storm had spent its strength. The wind was moderating. The twinkle of a star could be seen through a break in the overcast. And for the first time a little twilight could be seen on the distant horizons to the north. It was the turning of the tide of the night, when the sun started on its southward swing and the camp would take on new life as everyone realized that the worst of the winter night was behind us. Now we would turn our thoughts toward the trail, and I would be busy preparing for the longest dog-team trip of my life.

We assembled at breakfast to talk over the course of the day. The change in the weather allowed us to make one last search for the missing man.

Dick and I went to get on our warm clothes. We saw the door slowly opening, and a man stood there with only his eyes showing through the parka that was drawn closely around his face.

For a full minute no one moved. And no one uttered a sound as this ghostly figure covered with snow slowly made his way toward the now empty bunk.

No one helped him. Everyone seemed afraid to touch him. Then several of us moved at once.

I grabbed my knife and started cutting at the frozen parka, which was stiff as a board. His hands were swollen, his wrist-watch and identification tag having cut off the circulation. I split open the wrists of the rawhide mitts so we could pull them off. Meanwhile, the doctor was giving him hot coffee with whiskey in it. His toes were frozen and would have to be amputated, but we could not comprehend why he was not in worse condition.

When he could speak, he told us that he had kept walking as long as he could, and then he had dug a hole in the snow to sleep. When he woke, he went on again; then on Sunday morning it cleared, and he looked to the north and saw the first feeble ray of daylight.

No one knows for sure just what went on in his mind, but I have always believed that glimpse of the promise of daylight did it. Then turning around he saw the light on the tower of the camp, about three miles away, and headed for "home."

You cannot comprehend what light means to men who have lived in darkness, unless you have shared it with them. The hope of it brought new life and changed the morale of the entire camp.

Still, when word was finally passed around that the sun could actually be seen again, it failed to register at first. Men crawled out of their bunks as if walking in their sleep. They stared at the speaker in a daze, as if they could not grasp the meaning of what he had said. Then they rushed to see for themselves. Some went in the wrong direction, as if they did not know where they were going, and could not find the door. Only a few stopped to put on warm clothing, until the penetrating cold sent them quickly back again to do so.

The flaming red ball of fire looked like a cold red moon painted on the blackboard where a dark sky met the black waters of the Ross Sea.

Suddenly the air was rent by the voices of men in what was supposed to be a cheer. But it was more like the cry of creatures who had never seen such a thing before. It was as if we had been utterly ignorant that such a thing as the sun existed. We were like blind men whose sight had been suddenly restored.

The Antarctic night was not over, for the "days" were but a brief hour long. But the camp was transformed with a new spirit of life and activity. All my thoughts were now occupied in getting ready for the trail again. Sleds had to be lashed and gone over; new runners put on. Dog harnesses had to be made and fitted to the dogs, so they would not chafe. There was more seal blubber to be melted up for dog pemmican. Plans had to be made and discussed; lists of supplies made and checked.

The snow was cleared off the windows in the roof, and the lights were put out in the Mess Hall once a day, for a steadily increasing period. The dim, brief daylight which filtered through the glass made the room look like another world. But it was still cold, with winds of twenty to thirty miles, and temperatures down to 60° below. And all during this time we were getting news by radio from the United States about the heat wave that spread over the country and how many people were dying because of it.

How beautiful were the mornings now! How wonderful that daily glow from the rays of the sun on the northeastern horizon! Each day it was a bit longer, and its refracted and reflected colors were indescribable as the sunrise and the sunset slowly separated to give birth to a new day.

The sea smoke could be seen rising up over the Barrier. To the south it was still dark, like an overcast sky. To the northwest, West Cape could be seen standing out like a statue.

On August 22, when the sun rose completely above the horizon, a holiday was declared. We were all on hand to greet it as it rose, a red ball of fire seen for the first time in its full roundness. And though it was 50° below zero, our caps were off as the Stars and Stripes went up the flagpole again for the first time in four months.

But winter was not yet over. I took Gray Cloud for a run, and he was glad to get out; but very glad to get in again. It was 60° below when we skied to the pressure ice, looking for signs of seals. The snow sparkled like silver and the Barrier growled under enormous pressure.

The pressure ice heaved up on all sides, some of it twenty and thirty feet above the surface of the bay ice. There was continual cracking and groaning. I saw where a Weddell seal had crawled up through its blowhole on the ice, and its trail was marked with drops of blood, perhaps from having got caught in the pressure.

Suddenly I was startled by a tremendous explosion, as if the ice had been bombed. Fifty feet away from me tons of ice and snow shot up into the air. I looked out toward the mouth of the Bay of Whales and could see a great deal of sea smoke drifting away from the edge of the bay ice. This was proof that the water was open there—but it was still a long way out; it would be a long while before a ship could get through.

My mind was eager for the trail again, as it always has been when confined for any period of time. I was anxious to be heading out toward the mountains which had been seen from the air, but where no living man had been.

It was the last day of September when I took all of my dogs out of their tunnel for the first time, in order to get them in shape for the long trip. They were full of life and anxious to get going. We had plenty of weather to face, but the Antarctic night was over.

In fifteen days we would be heading southeast, maybe into a blizzard—but rising ever higher and higher above the horizon until at last it would encircle us daily without ever setting, would be the light-giving, life-giving sun.

9

WITH the return of the sun a new spirit of adventure stirred in us; I felt the restless urge of it in my very bones. It had been a long night and there was a long day ahead of us. Wherever we looked, we wanted to see over the next ridge or snow hill; we were eager to find what lay beyond.

Dick and I could hardly wait to get started on our long-contemplated trip with the dog teams which would take us into the eastern interior, the longest dog-sled trip ever made in Antarctica except for Amundsen's trip to the South Pole and back. We faced months of hard traveling through treacherous territory, over areas of crevasses and pitfalls, rough sastrugi and glare ice, tall haycocks and steep snow hills. It required extensive and very careful planning.

Every ounce of food for men and dogs had to be measured and weighed both with a view to the bulk and the weight of the loads we could carry and the proper proportions for each meal. We had to allow a safety factor for blizzards when we would be unable to travel and could only wait in our tent until it was over, consuming our precious provisions. We had to figure how far apart we would build our caches and what we would leave there, how many miles we would make each day with our heavy loads going out and our much lighter loads coming back again. We had to plan all this so we would not be caught on our return journey in a storm between caches, without adequate provisions. We went over and over every detail to be sure that we had not made any mistakes, for now was the time to discover any error in our planning, and not when we were five hundred miles out.

We took the sleds into the work house for a final going over. We had to be absolutely sure that our only means of transporting provisions would not fail us. The sleds were all hand-lashed to make them flexible, so they would ride easily with enough give on the rough surface we would often be obliged to sledge over. Every lashing that showed even the slightest sign of wear was replaced by a new one of the finest rawhide. Each gee-pole was planed down to the last shaving to save weight, but with care not to take off so much that it might weaken or break when strain was put on it to stop the team or push the sled. A gee-pole was lashed to the front of each sled to be used as a support when skiing beside it, and as a means of steering the sled when it required the whole weight and strength of one's body to pull it from one side or the other.

A new crutch rope was spliced into the sleds to be used as a bridle; and this had to be of the best, for all of the power which was supplied by the dogs in hauling the sled would pull through this crutch rope. The gang-line was tied to it, and the dogs would be fastened to the gang-line in pairs except for the lead dog, who pulled alone, out ahead. If the V-shaped crutch rope splice broke, the dogs might run away from us and the result might be serious. If a sled fell in a crevasse and the rope broke, we would lose all our provisions or all our dogs.

The harnesses, which were made of webbing, had to be gone over, one by one, and fitted to the dogs. The collar through which each dog pushed his head had to fit snugly and perfectly so that it would not chafe him or cut off his wind through days, weeks, and months of steady hauling up hill and down. Every one of these details was vital to the success of a sledging trip in Antarctica.

Everything we would need from the day we set out until the day we got back again had to be loaded on the sleds that two teams of nine dogs each could haul for us. The dog food had to be the very best that we could devise, and so rich that the dogs would need only a small portion of it daily to keep them in good shape. And we had to be absolutely sure of this, for it would be too late to prevent calamity if our dogs began to drop in their harness by the side of the trail, hundreds of miles from our base site. Many explorers before us had seen their dogs slowly starve to death, one by one, and had lost their lives because of lack of experience in planning and providing for them, their only means of transportation in the cold and desolate wastes of polar regions. We were determined that this should not happen to us. We considered all of the information and experience provided by men like Scott and Amundsen who had gone on before us; and I drew on all of my experience, which included life on the cold northern coast of Newfoundland as well as previous sledging trips in Antarctica.

Dick and I talked all this over many times before we decided exactly what to do. The very best food that you can give a dog in Arctic or Antarctic regions is that rich combination of meat and fat which is provided only by the seals of these same regions. Many a time in Newfoundland I had seen the noble sled dogs grow thin as they hauled from day to day on food other than seal meat. And I knew from experience that the fat or blubber from seals not only provided the nourishment a dog needs in polar regions, but also enabled him to grow a coat of silky fur to protect him in blizzards and bitterly cold weather. I had seen the slick look of beautiful Eskimo dogs with their soft, silky hair grown thick from eating the blubber of that useful polar mammal called the hair seal.

This was the seal meat we had been feeding to the dogs all through the winter. As a result, they were in good shape and their coats were glossy.

So while the kind of food was no problem, transporting it was. We could never haul the whole seal carcasses on our sleds, so we had to figure out some way of lightening the load without losing too much food value. We had been experimenting with this through the winter night and had hit upon a solution. Instead of taking the meat with its fat, we decided to take only the blubber. With a skinning knife, the hide and fat were separated from the lean meat, and then the fat was cut from the skin and thrown into an empty gasoline drum over a red-hot fire. Thus the blubber was melted down and made into oil, to which we added dog meal to give it bulk. After thorough mixing it was cast into molds that held just two pounds each; the amount each dog would be fed per day while on the trail. These two-pound blocks were frozen for ease in stacking on the sleds. We called this product "dog pemmican," and all our work in preparing it would save us much valuable time on the trail when we camped at night. It was easy to feed to our team, one block to each dog, and it saved the dogs much energy in eating it. All this was very important.

The man-food ration required equal care in planning. No man can last long traveling with a dog team in subzero temperatures without the proper nourishment. He slowly becomes weak from fatigue and finds himself in trouble before he realizes what is wrong with him.

The best food yet devised for polar travel was called "pemmican." The formula had been improved somewhat by the Americans, but it was originally made up by Roald Amundsen for use on his journey to the South Pole in 1911. It consisted of a combination of vegetables, meat, and fat—mostly fat, which is necessary to sustain body heat in polar regions. This was made up into cakes about three inches square which had only to be cut up in small pieces and dissolved in hot water. It then looked like pea soup and could be eaten with a spoon. Opinions differ with personal taste and conditions, but most of us found it very tasty when we first ate it. After a hard day on the trail, one cupful at night when we camped warmed us and stayed with us and made us feel comfortable. But after a long period we wished many a time that we had never seen the stuff; one soon becomes very tired of it as a steady diet.

With these food problems solved, our next problem was transportation: how to travel more than 1,200 miles by dog team with all the necessary equipment and provisions. The hundreds of pounds of food were only part of our load. The theodolite and tripod which Leonard Berlin would need for surveying were not light. The portable radio equipment, compass, tents, primus stoves, sleeping bags, extra clothing, and many other smaller necessary items ran into pounds, and every ounce meant more weight for the dogs to pull. We might be three or more months on the trail, and we had to provide for this.

Our objective was Hal Flood Mountain which was first seen by Admiral Byrd and photographed by aerial camera from a distance of eighty miles on our first expedition in 1929. In the picture, it looked like a big white cloud high above the horizon. We were not even sure that it was a mountain, because there have been many instances in which explorers have been wrong in their interpretation of what they have seen. But our trip lay in this direction and we had to figure on a distance of at least six hundred miles to reach our objective in Marie Byrd Land.

After much consideration, we decided to allow fifteen miles per day in going out with the heavier loads, and thirty miles per day on our way back again. We might make less or we might make more, but it gave us a basis for planning. So we proposed to build a cache every thirty miles and leave there enough food for both men and dogs to last two days. We would pick this up as we reached each cache on our way back, thus restocking our supplies for any weather emergencies; and this plan would enable us to lighten our outgoing load with every cache we laid down.

While we were completing these preparations, the tractor party hauling sleds with supplies made another attempt to reach the Rockefeller Mountains, a little over one hundred miles away, which would mark the first leg of our longer journey. I had no more faith in the success of this venture than I had had before, yet again I hoped I was wrong because she was to haul and cache dog food for us, and could be of great help.

We were one of three parties going into the field. The Geological Party and the Biological Party were going part way on the same trail with us, as far as the Rockefeller and McKinley mountains. We were the Pacific Coast Party who would survey the mountains beyond. There were to be three of us in our party, Dick Moulton and I, each with our own dog teams, doing all the sledging, and Leonard Berlin as the surveyor. In addition, I would double as the radioman and Dick as the cook.

The tractor party started out in 63° below zero weather and the next day radioed back that they were eighteen miles out but that they had had a lot of trouble with their load. The tractor sled had turned over three times, so they had already cached all the dog food, which would do us practically no good. They were proceeding, hauling only gasoline, to mark the trail for the army tank which would start as soon as they got near the mountains, and which, because it was so much faster, we expected would be able to get to the mountains and back before the tractor returned. Actually, after almost two weeks, the tractor party finally got within seven miles of the mountains, and were on their way back when the tank set out. The two parties met twenty-three miles out from base, the tank having had trouble with soft snow. It finally made sixty miles, dumped its load, and returned with its oil pump out of order. While both tank and tractor were intact and the men none the worse for their experience, their performance did not raise my hopes for the future of mechanized transport in Antarctica.

10

WEST Base was a bustle of activity as men went to and fro, their shadows pointing to the South Pole in the ever-rising sunlight. Each driver was busy with his team. New pups had to be broken to the harness and trained to travel with the veteran dogs. Short trips had to be made to get them used to hauling the sleds, and to harden them for the big loads. After being cooped up for months, with very little exercise, the dogs were glad to see the light of day and be out on the trail again. It was a job to put a team in harness after a period of inactivity. It was all one man could do to hitch them up, they were so full of energy and excitement. Many times the driver had to tie his sled fast before he began to harness his dogs. Then when they were all hitched up to the gang-line he grabbed his sled, slipped the line, and off they went like the wind with their tongues hanging out and their plumed tails curled up over their backs. There was nothing they enjoyed more than to gallop over the ice and snow on a cold frosty morning, following the lead dog who was guided by word of mouth from the driver.

Even the dogs seemed to feel the thrill of this teamwork. You tell your lead dog what to do, the way you want him to turn, and when you want him to stop. He understands and obeys immediately, and the rest of the team will follow him. A good lead dog is priceless; there are only a few of them. When you find a dog that will break trail without the driver going ahead of him, when he obeys your commands instantly as you steer by compass day after day over hundreds of miles of snow and sastrugi and glare ice, you have a good lead dog. If you lose the sled and he leaves you far behind, then suddenly looks back, stops and turns the team around to return to you, you have a leader who is also a friend. And if you can depend on his intelligence and judgment to lead you through the worst crevasse area in Antarctica without making a single mistake, you have a partner who is worth his weight in gold. St. Lunaire was like that; I have never found another dog to equal him. But King was one of the best at Little America III.

We were all anxious to be off, drawn on by the hidden mysteries that lay over the horizon in this unknown, icebound land. To make it still more interesting, a race was on to see who would be the first to reach the nearest range of mountains. Dick and I had been told in a nice way by new drivers of the other two parties that anyone could drive a team of dogs. All you had to do was to put them into harness, yell to them, and off they would go. Dick and I were both experienced dog drivers and we knew there was more to it than that, especially in the handling of dogs and the management of marches on a long sledging trip. We were determined to get to the mountains first, to show them the difference. We believed there is a great deal of difference between a good dog driver and a poor one. I have known men who have driven dogs all of their lives and are still not good drivers. You have to know and love your dogs and they have to feel this and return your love, if you are to get the most out of them. As the nearest mountains were about 125 miles away, with a two-day handicap that distance should reveal a difference between experienced and inexperienced trail driving.

The Biological Party, with Perkins in charge, left the base on the fifteenth of October, two days ahead of us. We wished Perkins all kinds of good luck, but felt sure we would pass him before he got to the Rockefeller Mountains. We said very little to anyone about this or about what we had in mind, but it got around camp that we had something up our sleeves.

One part of trail driving is to pack your loads to save time in camping. We loaded our sleds in such a way that the items necessary for making camp were on top. The rest could be left on the sled, tied up in the sled sheath to keep the snow from drifting in. Leonard and Dick and I each went over every article, checking and double checking; then, being satisfied that the loads were complete, we lashed them up. We put the tents on top, for they would be the first to come off and the last to go on after each trail camp.

Both the Geological Party and our Pacific Coast Party were scheduled to leave on October 17, but we didn't get started until late in the afternoon, so we were actually three days behind the Biological Party. It was 25° below zero. The wind was from the southeast and blowing directly in our faces. It took us a little time to get the dogs all in harness. They were as excited and raring to go as we were; I had all I could do to hold them. Every precious minute counted if we were to pass Perkins in a hundred miles with such a handicap.

At last everything was ready, the men were wishing us good luck, and the word was given to the dogs to be on their way. It did not have to be repeated; the dogs literally sprang into action, and though the loads were heavy, they had no trouble getting them into motion. Each of the two teams was hauling two sleds with a total weight per team of 1,400 pounds:

800 pounds on the front sled and 600 pounds on the tow-sled. But soon we were flying over the snow with the dogs' first mad excitement.

"Easy there, boys," I said. "You have a long way to go. Save that energy as much as possible."

They kept up their gallop for only a short distance and then slowly settled down to a more steady trot, for they were still shortwinded after their long winter confinement. The going was dry because of the low temperature; the snow was like powder and the runners dragged over it.

We had difficulty keeping from freezing. Low drift was flying over the Barrier, picked up by the wind, and slapping our faces like hailstones. When I removed my fur mitt to clear a dog harness, my hand immediately turned white and the fingers stiffened. I quickly put my mitt on again. The cold penetrated our very bones and the dogs were cold, too; they wanted to keep moving. What could we do without them? We knew that some of them might not survive such a long, hard journey as that which lay ahead of us; but we knew also that they would be faithful to the end. They depended on us as we did on them; and in their every whine, howl, and bark they told us that they would not let us down if they could help it.

Ahead of us lay adventure, danger, and silence. There would be monotonous days of traveling over a bitterly cold and seemingly endless waste, but the passing hours and endless days do not lower the spirit of the proud Eskimo dog; he travels gaily along pulling the sled, and with his pricked-up ears and beautiful tail high above his back, he is something to behold and remember forever. We were proud of our dogs and loved every one of them. They were doing good work, pulling heavy loads against a strong wind. We decided that seven miles was enough for the first march, having started so late in the day.

We worked out a system for camping that would save us time later. We watched for a level surface and stopped the dogs right on their trail; making no detour for a camp site. We unlashed the two tents and staked them out end to end and according to the direction of the wind, with the hole to crawl through in the lee. Then Dick and I went to our dogs and unharnessed them, chaining them to the tethering line which we fastened to pegs driven into the snow. Leonard got our sleeping bags off the sleds and pushed them through the hole into the tent. We then fed our dogs their two pounds of pemmican each. How proud they looked as they watched us coming toward them with their food. Their tails would wag and their bold-looking eyes and faces were eloquent with pleasure and appreciation.

Many times they did not feel satisfied, and would look at us, asking for more. I would say to King, "That is all, old boy. We can't give you any more. You will have to get along with it."

He would understand the tone of voice if not the words, and set the example by licking up every crumb, after which he was ready to lie down for the night. I would then take my small shovel and dig a hole for each dog, just big enough for him to curl up in. Now he was protected from the wind and could sleep comfortably. In soft snow the dogs would rather do this themselves, but in hard snow they always looked expectantly for me to do it for them. When I was through, each one would look up at me as if to say "Thank you," and then lie down, curling his tail snugly around his nose.

Dick got into his tent and set up a primus stove to warm our pemmican while Leonard brought snow for him to melt. I set up the radio, running out my antenna on skis which I used for poles. Leonard arranged the sleeping bags in the tents, his and mine in one tent with the radio and Dick's in the other, which was our mess tent. Dick was working on our meal while we were busy getting the tents in order. Then Dick would sing out, "Come and get it!" and we would eat and talk things over together.

When the utensils were cleared away the three of us would go into the radio tent to hold our schedule with the base, give our daily report, and hear the news in return. Then I would tune in on the schedules of other field parties, especially Perkins and the Biological Party, so we would know where they were and what chance we still had of overtaking them.

On October 20 we were thirty miles out from Little America and Warner of the Geological Party was ten miles behind us. Perkins, with his three-day head start, was out sixty miles.

The going was hard again, for the temperature was low, but the dogs were handling the loads adequately and getting used to it. The Geological Party was making slow progress. They stayed in their tents one whole day because of a blizzard, but we made ten miles.

The tank, which left shortly after Perkins, was already at the mountains. The news from the red tractor, which was following us, said that they were going in reverse. This meant that the snow was ridgy and criss-crossed with sastrugi; and with its heavy tow it was too dangerous to go ahead for fear of turning over on end. This also meant that the tractor was making only two miles per hour, which seemed like pretty slow going; yet it was faster than the dog teams at this period, and with little effort on the part of the men. Boyd, who was in charge, skied most of the time. At night the men did not have to make camp like the dog-team parties, for they were towing a small house which they used for shelter, sleeping, and cooking.

On the twenty-second we were out sixty-two miles and could just see the Rockefeller Mountains in the distance. The Geo-

logical Party was out thirty-nine miles, and we had not heard
from the Biological Party. On the twenty-third I learned over
the radio that the Biological Party had made only seventeen
miles to our twenty, which meant that we had gained some that
day. This put us out eighty-two miles. I was very anxious to
hear the news from the Biological Party that evening because
we did not know where they were, except that they must be
getting pretty close to the mountains. We would have to catch
them soon if we were going to.

After I had signed off on my schedule with Little America,
I turned my dial to the wave length Perkins was using. After
a little shifting back and forth, I finally got him and listened
in on a very interesting conversation. Perkins was being congratulated on the splendid day's run he had made, which put
him within eleven miles of the mountains. He was told that the
Pacific Coast Party was hot on his heels, but they could not
catch him now because at the end of that day's run they were
seventeen miles back of him.

"Congratulations," the voice said again. "You have done
a good job and you will be the first to reach the mountains."

We sat around the radio that evening, feeling a bit weary
from the twenty miles we had traveled that day at 22° below
zero. All was quiet outside; the dogs were sleeping soundly,
and the tents were steady in the breeze. We were about ready
to crawl into our sleeping bags when I stopped fiddling with
the radio and took off the earphones. I looked at Dick and Leonard, wondering what their reaction would be when I told them
what I had just overheard. They looked at me sleepily but expectantly, and then the weariness dropped from their faces as
they saw the expression upon mine.

"Let's have it, Jack."

"What did you hear?"

As I told them, sleep was forgotten. We started figuring out how we could still get to the mountains before the Biological Party. It had to be now or never; this was our last chance. Dick and I thought our dogs could make it if we let them rest until midnight. If we started then, we estimated we would pass Perkins around 6:00 A.M. From there it would be easy enough to make the remaining eleven miles to the mountains in two or three hours.

At midnight we were laughing over a pot of hot pemmican, thinking of how surprised Perkins would be when he crossed our trail next day on his trip in. The temperature had gone down to 45° below and it felt bitterly cold. We dressed in our furs and had the tents down and all the equipment lashed on the sled before we disturbed the dogs. At the last minute, Dick and I decided to put our teams together, eighteen dogs hauling one double load, so there would be no waiting when once we got started.

I spoke to my dogs, saying, "It's now or never, boys. This is your chance to prove your worth, the one time you are called on to help out."

They looked at me with half-open eyes, then raised their heads, yawned, and snuggled down again. They were so comfortable curled up in the snow that they did not want to be disturbed. But I took them one by one, patting them on the head, and put them in harness. Dick was doing the same with his dogs, while Leonard was looking over the camp site to be sure that we had everything.

By this time all the dogs sensed that something special was going on. It was cold and they wanted to warm up. When we gave the word, they were off at a good clip, springing forward into their harnesses. The wind dropped down to a dead calm and all was quiet except for the sound of the sled runners breaking through the crust of snow. Dick and I were talking to our dogs, encouraging them in that jargon which only dogs can understand. We were telling them that once we got to the mountains a long rest awaited them. They picked up a pace as if they understood us, and I think they did.

In the early morning we came to bad ice, frozen high over the snow in a shell which the dogs broke through. It slowed them down, yet did not stop our progress. Soon after seven miles we struck good going again and traveled easily at a fast walk.

At exactly the time we had figured, we rose over a high snow hill and saw straight ahead of us in a low valley the tents of the Biological Party. We stopped and gave the dogs a short rest while we talked over the situation. Should we go straight by them, or make a little detour? If we drove close to the tents, their dogs would bark at ours and Perkins would see us. He might then still beat us to the mountains because his dogs would be fresh and rested and his loads were light; the tank had relieved him of some of them.

We all voted to detour a half mile to one side of the camp where Perkins and his party were still sleeping. We proceeded slowly, talking very low to our dogs and holding our breaths for fear of attracting the dogs of the Biological Party. If they all started barking, someone would be sure to look out and see us. One of the dogs did bark a few times, but the rest paid no attention and evidently none of the men did, either.

When we had sledged over a ridge where they could no longer see us, we headed straight on our course again. Eleven more miles brought us to Tank Depot 105. Boyd saw us coming, but was sure it was the Biological Party until, with surprise, he recognized us. The radioman, just then in contact with Little America, was asked if the Biological Party had arrived yet.

"No," he said, "but the Pacific Coast Party is here." Little America signed off; no comment.

Between 8:00 A.M. on the twenty-third and 8:00 A.M. on the twenty-fourth, we had traveled forty-five miles.

We immediately made camp to give our dogs the long day of rest which they had so well earned. Perkins came in seven hours later, at 3:00 P.M., very much surprised to find us already there. We heard no more about how easy it was to be a good dog driver.

11

ON the twenty-sixth, while we were still waiting for the Geological Party to catch up with us, Dick and I went on skis to climb Tennant Peak, named after George Tennant, our cook on the first Byrd Expedition, in the Rockefeller Mountains. It was a beautiful day and the visibility was of the best. Every ridge on the Barrier and every peak rising high above the glacial ice in the mountain range could be clearly seen. We anticipated no difficulty, but as we ascended higher and higher, the going got tricky. We took off our skis and used them to make holes for footing. We had no rope to trust to, no alpine ax to cut our way; we were just carefree men out adventuring.

The first ridge we came to was covered over with glacial ice except for a few bare rocks. The next one was steeper and every step had to be taken with care, every foothold had to be sure, for one slip would be enough. After many near slips, we reached the summit.

Luck was with us; there was no wind. Had there been, we would have been in a dangerous position, for no one could hold fast to the ice-coated rocks in an Antarctic blizzard. But we had not thought of this while climbing, nor did we think of it while getting our breath at the top, looking out into space over the millions of tons of snow and ice that blanketed this silent, unexplored region of the great Antarctic continent. To the north of us lay miles of ice and open space extending to the Ross Sea. To the south lay mountain peaks and plateaus leading toward the South Pole. To the west lay Little America, a tiny dot on the great Ross Ice Shelf, more than a hundred miles away. And to the east lay unknown territory and the mountains which were our goal, five hundred miles away.

We looked in awe over this silent domain. Every snow hill, every wave in the Barrier ice, could be seen distinctly, and further down the mountain, the silvery snow glistened in the sunlight.

Time seemed to stop in the aura of these mountain peaks which rose out of the glacial ice in which they had been buried for fifty thousand years or more. Far away beyond the northern horizon was a world full of people whom we had known all our lives; our homes were there, and all our loved ones, yet in this lonely spot their existence seemed unreal.

We broke away from the silent grip that held us with a sudden realization that our descent would be more difficult than our climb, and that we must get down before the wind rose. We steadied ourselves over the first ridge downwards, using our skis as much as possible for brakes. We dared not let them slip out of our hands, for they would go down the mountain like a streak. If we lost or broke them it would be a long, weary walk back to camp.

Slowly we picked each step until we reached the less steep glacial incline. There we could breathe easier, and sit on our skis which we used as sleds, sailing down the long incline to level ice and good ski surface. From there we skied into camp, arriving at 10:00 P.M. tired and hungry but satisfied, the first to climb Tennant Peak.

It was the twenty-eighth before the Geological Party came in. Warner, the leader, was all smiles as he talked about his dogs and the trip.

"That lead dog of mine," he said, "will do just the opposite of what I tell him to do. When I say Haw, he goes Gee."

A site was picked out near Franklin Peak for the three men who were going to spend the summer there to collect data. To supply their camp meant a hard pull for the dog teams up the glacier, so Dick and I were going to help them with it.

The dogs were feeling good after their long rest and were anxious to get into harness again. We started out with heavily loaded sleds and had gone only a little way when we came to an open crevasse, black and ugly. Luckily we saw it just before we reached it, a black hole dropping down to darkness and surrounded by a thinly covered shell of snow and ice that no sled could cross over safely. We picked our way around it over safer ice; it was all hollow underneath, but the bridge held us.

We came then to the beginning of the glacier and started to climb it. It was hard for the dogs to get a footing on the ice. Our skis were slipping, too, and if we hadn't had the support from the gee-pole of our sleds we could not have stayed on our feet at all.

At midnight we were half way up, taking it slowly and resting our dogs often. The midnight sun was high in the heavens, but there was a haze over it so we could not see it plainly. The air was still, and although we enjoyed the mountain scenery, it was a hard pull. We were finally forced to take off our skis, put crampons on our feet, and haul with the dogs in order to make it. But I wouldn't have had it any different. This was the life for me—out in the wide open spaces of Antarctica, fighting the glacial elements of an ice age with the very best of men and loyal dogs for companions.

We delivered our loads and made a quick descent to the foot of the glacier, where we stopped to see the remains of the Fokker plane that had been wrecked in 1929 on our first expedition, still there after eleven years of Antarctic blizzard buffeting. We each took a souvenir from the wing, then went on to camp in a twenty-mile wind with low drift. Looking back, the mountains were invisible. The snow picked up by the wind from the Barrier had drawn a curtain between us.

Our loads were now sorted again and packed for the next leg of our journey to the McKinley Mountains, which Admiral Byrd had discovered in 1929. The Geological and Biological parties, with the tractor party to help them, were going as far as Mount Grace McKinley, 120 miles away. We were all to leave the Rockefeller Mountains together. Dick and Leonard and I were to lead the trail and look for the best route to avoid crevasses for the tractor which was, among other things, hauling dog pemmican for us as far as Mount Grace McKinley. Meanwhile, our own loads having been lightened by laying caches and consuming food, Dick's extra tow-sled and mine were both loaded with supplies for the other parties who would leave us at the McKinley Mountains. Beyond that we were proceeding alone.

We pulled out of Depot 105 on November 1, with the tractor following us, and camped that night near the foot of the plateau on which we proposed to travel. We couldn't see how steep it was, for the visibility had closed in and completely obliterated our view.

In the morning we reached the plateau after two miles of hauling and one detour the tractor took around a crevasse. By resting the dogs at intervals, we got up the incline of a snow ramp without too much trouble. Then we traveled eastward on the plateau and had gone about eight miles when we were startled by a terrific roaring, as if the whole Barrier were splitting apart, and the ice began to shake beneath us. We all stopped, men and dogs standing perfectly still. The roaring was continuous, coming toward us at first from the south; we could hear it traveling fast and getting closer. The dogs crouched, bellies to the snow, shivering. The men were tense and speechless. A cold chill started up my spine and I am sure that the rest felt the same way. Was the ice breaking up underneath us? We had heard nothing like this before. It passed by us, an unseen yet tangible thing, on its way to the north, and the cannonlike roar could be heard long after it went by, traveling on in the far distance.

"What was that?" we asked each other. "An earthquake?"

None of us had ever experienced such a phenomenon, but it was the only thing we could think of. It was, in any case, an icequake. Some great disturbance had caused the ice of the great plateau and Barrier to shiver and shake for at least sixty seconds. We could still hear the echo like distant thunder.

We camped where we were and in our radio message to Dr. Paul Siple, who was in charge of the base at Little America, we reported, "Earthquake of minute duration hit here at 5:15."

The next three days we made good time on the plateau: the surface was good and the dogs were doing splendidly. We established our first two depots on the McKinley trail, thirty and sixty miles from the Rockefeller Mountains, depositing man and dog food that we would use on our return trip.

The next thirty miles were hard going, and it took us three days to make it. We traveled over many rough patches of sastrugi that made the sleds groan and twist under the heavy loads. To further plague us, the wind blew all night, then a white mist set in so we could not navigate. And just as we were putting our tents up, a blizzard suddenly came down. We hurried to bank the tents with snow, driving the pegs in deep, and to feed the dogs and dig holes to give them shelter. The wind howled all night, and the tents rattled as if they would split apart, but the tent pegs held in the snow. We stayed in our sleeping bags all the next day, crawling out only long enough to eat and care for the dogs, who were comfortable in their warm beds of snow. The day after, the sun came out but was soon blanketed by a heavy fog blown in by a strong wind. The going was hard, with the wind directly in our faces, as we crossed the 150th meridian and built our ninety-mile cache. The meter wheel—a bicycle wheel trailing behind the sleds for the purpose of recording mileage—registered 232 miles since leaving Little America.

We were now in the territory which we had set out to survey and claim for the United States of America as having been discovered by Admiral Byrd on previous expeditions. The Rockefeller Mountains and the region through which we had been traveling up to the 150th meridian were considered to be British territory.

The next two days the going was rugged. As I was descending a steep snow hill my rear sled tipped over, but luckily the load was securely lashed so I lost nothing. We all had many spills on that hill, and the tractor zigzagged down it for fear of turning over.

Now we could see Mount Grace McKinley in the distance, snowtopped and covered over with glacial ice except for a ridge of bare rock on the north side. The next day we camped at the mountain's foot, staked out our dogs, and immediately started to climb it. Our hope was to find the cairn built by the Eastern Marie Byrd Land Party of the Second Byrd Antarctic Expedi-
wine which we were anxious to claim. The mountain was steep,
tion in 1934. We knew that they had left in it a bottle of sherry

but we reached the ridge without mishap and saw the cairn
a little distance away, a pile of granite rocks five feet high with
only a little snow on them even after six years. When we took
the cairn apart we found the bottle of wine, some food, and
a note. I took great care in bringing that bottle down the icy
mountain and opened it only after the Biological, Geological,
and tractor parties were gathered together so we could all
share it.

In the note there was a description of the work done in
this region by the Eastern Marie Byrd Land Party which made
a geological, botanical, and biological survey of the unknown
territory to the north and east of Mount Grace McKinley. "This
cairn," the report stated, "was erected by us on December 10,
1934, with every hope that those finding it can make use of
the contents to advantage and also a silent expression of our
thoughts for future explorers in this area and the sincere hope
that their trip will be as enjoyable and fruitful as ours has
been." It was signed by Paul A. Siple, Erie, Pa.; Stevenson
Corey, Winchester, Mass.; A. Alton Wade, Baltimore, Md.; and
O. Tan Cliff, Erie, Pa., U.S.A.

It was now our mission, in 1940, to make the first survey
and for the first time in history to stake and claim land in
Antarctica for the United States. We chained the base of the
mountain for a triangulation to shoot an angle for the brass
monument we were to build on the cairn. Leonard Berlin set
up his theodolite and tripod to get interval observations of the
sun to establish the position of the mountain. Len was almost
freezing, beating his hands together to keep them from getting
stiff as he read off the angles, while I was keeping the time
in the tent.

That done, we climbed the mountain again to build another cairn in which to deposit our report, which included the

surveying data and the witnessed statement of the time and date when the claim was made. I had my movie camera sitting on the rocks to take a picture of our little ceremony as with bared heads we all shook hands while I held the Stars and Stripes above the brass survey cap. Over this we built the cairn of rocks, setting the flag on top of it.

It was a cold ceremony in a twenty-mile wind that forced us to cling to the rocks and ice on our way down to keep from being blown off. But as we looked back and saw the American flag flying in triumph on top of this lone mountain at the bottom of the world, we may be excused for a warm feeling of pride and a memory which will never be forgotten.

12

AFTER sending a radiogram to Commissioner Johnson of the General Land Office in Washington reporting our first claim, we made ready for the long sledging trip of more than three hundred miles which still lay ahead of us. Leonard and Dick and I, the Pacific Coast Party, were proceeding alone into unknown territory from Mount Grace McKinley. The other parties were remaining in the region between the McKinleys and Mount Rea.

We broke camp after taking on fourteen bags of dog pemmican weighing sixty-three pounds each. This was all we could carry in addition to what we had, and we would have to make it do. Our total loads now weighed around 1,400 pounds for each team, divided between the two sleds which each team was still hauling. We started out surrounded by mountain peaks and beauty such as we had never seen on the bleak Barrier. Snowy petrels flew around us, pretty things on the wing, their white bodies set off by black feet and beak. From our second camp by the airplane cache at Mount Rea we would be making new tracks on the white "sands of time" in this eternal land. This called for a celebration. We made Sunday a day of rest, and for supper that night we feasted on bouillon, bacon, tea, honey, and fancy cookies which had been saved for such an occasion.

On the top of Mount Rea's bold-looking landscape was a large craterlike hole, which looked as if a metal sphere had fallen there in the far past and then disappeared. We left camp on a rise of sastrugi running north from the mountain's steep cliffs. After dropping over this rough piece of surface, we had fair going down a smooth grade to the beginning of the valley where we started to ascend again, quite sharply, toward a region of upheaved ice islands and hundreds of crevasses.

We kept to the east side of this disturbance and made the grade over deep sastrugi and rough spots where the snow broke underneath our sleds, followed by a stretch of slippery glass ice, devoid of snow. That night we camped halfway through the valley on a thin patch of snow no larger than a rug. We found it very difficult to stake out our dogs and put up the tents, for we could not get the tent pegs driven into the ice. We were in a bad spot if a blizzard should blow up, but there was nothing we could do about it.

The next morning we pulled out as quickly as we could. The dogs were slipping and clawing at the ice, and it was almost impossible to get a footing on our skis. Every puff of wind carried us either sideways or backwards, according to its direction. In many places the ice was frozen in waves which made it very hard on the dogs, for we would suddenly go down in a trough on a fast run and stop short on the upward move to the crest.

To the east of us, as we ascended, was a mountain in the Edsel Ford Range. The ice was pushed out over its edge so that it looked like Niagara Falls. When we neared the end of the valley, a distance of almost twenty miles, we came to thin surface snow and very wide crevasses, actually more like big chasms bridged over with snow. We hesitated many times before venturing over them, but luck was with us and we did not break through once. That night we camped between two mountains where our radio was unable to contact the base for our radio schedule.

We gave the valley an obvious but apt name, Crevasse Valley. One crevasse was so large it blocked our way entirely, and as we tried to get around it, at the critical moment King decided to travel parallel with the crevasse instead of across it. Only by instantly stopping the teams did I avoid a break-through.

We were traveling over No-man's Land and were conscious of the thrill of it as we followed our course into the unknown. We were gaining elevation all the time, and by the time we were sixty miles out, building Cache No. 2 on our new Hal Flood trail, we were up about 6,000 feet. The dogs were getting thin and I began to worry about them. If they gave out, we were done for.

Next day it began to snow and blow. The going would be hard, so Dick and I decided to put our teams together. We had gone about seven miles when one of my black wolf dogs, Prince, gave out and I had to haul him on my sled, hoping he would recover. We camped in a howling blizzard which kept us in our tents all the next day, but gave the dogs a chance to rest. On the radio schedule I received a message from Ada; all was well at home nine thousand miles away. We were also informed from the base that Leonard and I were scheduled to go home on the *North Star* after we got back, and Dick on the *Bear*. When we looked out of our tents we could not even see our dogs; they were drifted over with snow.

By morning the blizzard had abated, but after we broke camp and dug our dogs and sleds out of the snow we were traveling in an opaque mist little better than darkness. All the dogs began to show signs of exhaustion. Prince was on his feet again, but poor Bo was stumbling along. I felt very sorry for him for he was getting awfully thin, yet there was nothing I could do about it. It was essential to keep the dogs on their feet because we had a long way to go and the failure of one dog would make it all the harder on the others. We were still going upgrade; when we once gained the top of the mountainous plateau they would have an easier time. We rested them often and finally camped for a whole day because the visibility was zero.

Next morning the clouds began to part and patches of blue sky could be seen. At three o'clock in the afternoon the visibility opened up ahead of us and we could see for miles. We found ourselves near the crest of the rise. Straight ahead of us on the horizon we saw what looked like a big white cloud, but as it remained stationary, we decided it had to be the 10,000-foot Hal Flood Mountain our destination. The blood coursed faster in our veins and our growing discouragement vanished. It was still a long way off and we could only guess at the distance. Leonard guessed sixty miles, Dick fifty, and I out of wishful thinking made it forty-five miles.

We hadn't gone very much farther when we found that our dogs could hardly haul the sleds. The situation looked serious. I decided to leave my rear sled behind, stuck up in the snow, and Dick and I then put our dogs together in one team again. This helped, but in spite of a down grade, we made only ten miles. Next day we went slowly onward in a white mist that reduced visibility to zero. Prince gave out again and I hauled him on the sled for ten miles. By evening the air cleared and we could see the horizon about us, but there was no sign of Hal Flood Mountain. We figured that we must be down in a hollow, for we could not have made such a mistake. We were all certain that we had seen it, but now everything looked perfectly flat. A snowy petrel flew over us, circled around a few times as if investigating us, and then sailed straight ahead of us toward the mountain that ought to be there if we had not been seeing things. Again this encouraged us, like an omen.

The only sensible thing to do when a dog gives out on a trail hundreds of miles from your base is to kill him mercifully. But I hauled Prince on, unwilling to part with him or start killing dogs before we had even reached our destination. We were going over long grades and up and down over snow hills. Nine more snowy petrels encircled us, and this was almost a sure sign of mountains.

On our radio schedule we were asked about the condition of our dogs; complaints had been coming in from Perkins' party back at the McKinley Mountains that their dogs were in bad shape. One block of pemmican was evidently not enough to sustain the dogs under hard going when hauling heavy loads, but we could not have hauled any more, and had to make the pre-arranged rations last. Poor Prince was hauling again, pulling hard and doing his best, but he could not stand the gaff very long at a time. He would never be able to make the long trip back to the base.

By another evening the sun came through the clouds and we could see the horizon with what looked like a white mountain still ahead of us, but very much larger than our first sight of it. Excitement kept me from sleeping that night. I kept sticking my head out through the hole in the tent to see if it was still there, and to enjoy the great sight of that towering white monster with its head in the sky.

On December 1 we had to help our dogs haul through heavy, soft snow and made only three miles. But there the mountain was ahead of us; there could be no question about it now. We had traveled forty-five miles since we first saw it, but there were still fourteen or fifteen miles to go, so Leonard had been right. We laid down a base line of 24,000 feet so Len could get a triangular shot at the mountain peak. But we had gone only 9,000 feet when a blizzard came up and we had to head for camp until the weather cleared. Our ski trail was covered over and we could hardly see the flags we had laid. It took us over an hour to find our tents again.

We spent three days chaining the 24,000 feet, and during that time the peaks of the mountain were obliterated by fog and cloud banks. When the fog lifted, we saw that Hal Flood was the largest mountain of any we had seen thus far. It was covered with ice except to the north, where black rock was visible. There were three more ridges south of the mountain itself, and about sixty miles to the north was another mountain, not shown on the maps. This one was our own discovery.

The temperature went up to 36° above when the sun came out. It was the warmest we had experienced; the dogs lay stretched out full length on the snow and we were going about our work stripped to the waist.

After Leonard had completed his survey and latitude observations, we cached all the unnecessary gear, and sledged fourteen miles to the foot of Hal Flood, where we camped for the night.

We got up early and set out to climb the mountain with cameras, crampons, specimen bags, alpine rope, and the American flag. It took us hours to climb a rock ridge on the north side. The mountain was of volcanic formation and basaltic rock. We found dirt and mud, and collected fungus and rock specimens. Then we built a cairn over the survey cap identifying the location and deposited a report of our claim, topping it with the U.S. flag. We left a box of cigarettes in the cairn with a note telling the next party who would find it to have a smoke on us, the first three men who had ever set foot on this land. (Actually, this peak is no longer shown on maps as Mount Hal Flood, since that name has now been given to the mountain range.)

Now our mission was over, and we faced a long, hard journey back. As soon as we left the foot of the mountain Prince fell flat in his harness. The poor fellow had made the goal, but he could not go back. As I just couldn't bring myself to kill him, Dick offered to do the job. He led Prince off the trail, and the report of his .45 went through me like a knife. Now we had only seventeen dogs, but we were homeward bound.

At the end of another day Bo, too, fell down in his harness, but I put him on my sled and gave him a lift. After resting he was able to keep on his feet all the next day, but at sixty miles he gave out again. Next morning Dick found one of his dogs dead when he went to put him in harness. We fed the remaining sixteen dogs an extra daily ration out of our own supply of crackers. They sensed that we were on the way home and were running against time. When we reached Mount Rea, another of Dick's dogs died. We learned from the base by radio that Paul Siple and Ted Petres had made a flight to Hal Flood on the first day when visibility permitted, but they could not see us to drop food.

The Beechcraft plane flew over us now and headed for the Mount Rea airplane cache. When we got there the plane had gone, but the Geological Party was waiting for us and Paul had left a ham, fruit, and two loaves of bread for us. We had a long way still to go, but the sight of four friends and the dinner we had together made us feel as if we had already reached civilization. From here on the Geological Party would travel with us.

Our second day out, Bo just lay down, unable to go any

further. He had given us all he had, another sacrifice to man. Dick and I now had only seven dogs apiece.

At Mount Grace McKinley we met the tractor party, and Boyd had a big stew waiting for us in the caboose. We blessed him for that; I never tasted anything so good. We were completely tired out and my leg, which I had somehow strained during the long ski journey, pained so I could hardly sleep.

When we left the McKinleys, my dog Blackie gave out and a day later he died. This was a shock because he had always been one of the best and strongest. By the time we reached the Rockefeller Mountains two more of my dogs, Duke and White, showed signs of weakness. When Duke collapsed, Larry Warner of the Geological Party hauled him on his sled to give him another chance. The wolf dogs did not have the stamina of the Eskimo husky. King was still going strong, and my little Siberian husky, Gray Cloud, was keeping up with him.

On Christmas day the tractor broke through into a crevasse, but fortunately the crevasse was not big enough to swallow it completely. It took us a day to fill up a bridge beneath the tractor and dig her out again.

On New Year's Eve we were camping on the Ross Ice Shelf. The dogs made an awful commotion, which was unusual on the trail because they were always so tired they curled up and went right to sleep. We made a wild rush for the hole in the tent to see what was causing all the trouble. An Adélie penguin had walked into camp and was dancing around the dogs just out of their reach. They were doing their best to get hold of him, for he was fresh meat and they were hungry. Harold Gilmour caught him to add the skin to his personal collection, and the dogs had their meal.

We hadn't seen the sun for more than two weeks, but it broke through with the New Year; the temperature went up and the snow became sticky and difficult to traverse. The wind was in our favor, however, so Dick and I used our tents as sails to make it easier for the dogs. The sun made us all feel better, and the sight of a Wilson petrel and a skua gull broke the monotony, gracefully symbolizing life in a dead world.

In the morning we were awakened by the roar of an airplane engine. When I looked out of the tenthole it was foggy again, but soon a plane was soaring over us. It was the Condor, flying out to the tractor before bringing us some much-needed seal meat that had been promised for our dogs.

A little later we heard another roar, and this time it was the Beechcraft which circled us and then landed. The pilots brought us two bags of seal meat and told us that the Condor had been forced down ten miles away with a broken cylinder. The plane would have to be abandoned, and they were on the way to pick up her crew.

On the sixth of January we arrived at Aurora Camp, fourteen miles from West Base. Another day would see us in, so we took time out to wash and shave and clean up for our arrival, something that had never been done before on previous expeditions. The trail parties usually came in with full beards and so dirty they would stick to the first thing they touched. The Pacific Coast Party was going to be one outfit that came into camp from the longest, hardest trip of all as spruced up as we had left it.

Next day our twelve remaining dogs raced into camp, all in surprisingly good condition after sledging 1,220 miles. Gray Cloud came through with flying colors to return home with us. We had been gone eighty-three days. It was early in the morning and everyone was still asleep, but Charlie Shirley was soon out with his camera to get a photographic record of the event. Next to Amundsen's polar journey, it was the longest sledging trip that had ever been made in Antarctica; and it was the last of its kind. The man-and-dog sledging era of long-distance Antarctic exploration was over. Planes, helicopters, and tractors would now take over in the future inevitable march of scientific progress. Man and machines instead of man and dogs would now be pitted against the Antarctic ice. Civilization had already begun to invade Antarctica; the days of primitive pioneering adventure were done. Polar exploration in the Great White South would never more be the same.

"Jack," said Charlie, "you look thin. Where did you leave it?"

I went in the house and weighed myself. I had lost twenty pounds.

part IV

RECONNAISSANCE
PARTY

Operation Deepfreeze / 1955–57

1

THE U.S. Antarctic Service Expedition of 1939–41 closed its logbook without a further continuation of the Antarctic studies under Admiral Byrd because Congress refused to appropriate any more money. The work that had been done was regarded as of great importance in obtaining information and data on the Antarctic which had been unknown before. More than half of the total coast line of Antarctica and large sections of the interior had been mapped by means of aerial photography. Magnetic, seismographic, meteorological, geological, biological, and topographical data had been collected to supplement and extend previous studies as well as to contribute new discoveries. Our long ground survey trip by dog team had provided base lines and key points for mapping purposes as well as establishing priority of claim for land and mountains previously discovered by Admiral Byrd. In recognition of our services, three mountains bear the names of Leonard, Dick, and myself: Mount Berlin, Mount Moulton, and Mount Bursey.

But the world was in a turmoil and Congress did not feel that any more money should be expended in Antarctica when the United States was in danger of being involved in another war. When this expectation materialized, I enlisted in the United

States Coast Guard in 1942, serving first in the North Atlantic region and then in the Pacific as Commanding Officer of Ship *FS-269*, Philippine Islands.

After the war was over, and while I was still in the U.S. Coast Guard, the challenge of Antarctica was again taken up under Admiral Byrd's leadership, this time by the United States Navy as a part of its training and research activities. The 1946–47 U.S. Navy Antarctic Expedition, called Operation Highjump, was the largest exploring expedition that had ever been organized. With its fleet of thirteen ships and four thousand men, including a few Army and civilian observers and scientists, it brought all the resources of science to bear upon a complete encircling reconnaissance of the Antarctic continent as well as inland photographic excursions by plane. Many new developments had come out of the war, including the 6,600-ton, 10,000-h.p. Coast Guard icebreaker *Northwind* and the Navy's *Burton Island*. All these developments were put under test in Operation Highjump to discover and overcome their defects for use in polar regions. Besides fulfilling the purpose of geographic discovery, the expedition was a sort of grand rehearsal for the launching of a new era of completely mechanized exploration. The Heroic and Adventurous Ages of polar exploration were over.

I was not released from active duty in the U.S. Coast Guard Reserve until 1946 and so did not take part in Operation Highjump. Then I was recalled to active duty in 1951, and accompanied three Arctic missions as navigating officer of the U.S. icebreaker *Northwind,* which had bucked the southern ice pack on the U.S. Navy Antarctic Expedition.

When I was again released from active duty in 1954, I thought I would stay home and settle down at last. I had had enough of snow and ice in both the Arctic and the Antarctic regions. But when I read about another Antarctic expedition that was shaping up in Washington, my blood began to boil once more. The greatest of all expeditions was preparing to sail south to the bottom of the world, and I couldn't get it out of my mind. It haunted my dreams at night and my thoughts by day for weeks on end, until at last I paced the floor, unable to sit still for a minute.

"I wish you would sit down, darling," Ada would say to me. "You're making me nervous, pacing back and forth like that. What's wrong?"

All this had happened before, many times, in our married life and Ada knew well enough what was wrong with me; only she wanted me to make my decision and get it over with. She understood the compulsive spirit of adventure that kept pushing me forward inch by inch, until I could make up my mind. She said nothing to influence me, one way or the other. She had stood by my every other decision; and even though she might wish or think that I should settle down, we both knew I would have to decide it within myself.

It was not just desire of adventure, because I dreaded the thought of leaving home for another two years. And I had a good home, a wonderful wife and daughter, and a cottage on the lake where I could lounge in summer comfort while the Antarctic blizzards were howling. But there was only one thing I could do to escape the unrelenting drive within me. I had to apply for a passage.

So I wrote to Admiral Byrd requesting that I be allowed to sail on the *Atka,* a ship that was setting forth on a reconnaissance expedition to the Antarctic. But all the billets on the *Atka* were filled, and no more room was available. I was disappointed, but the Admiral told me that a greater expedition was sailing the following year. He advised me to wait for it, and suggested that I write to Admiral Dufek who was in command of Task Force 43, and who would lead the expedition.

This warmed my heart and eased the tension, for Admiral Dufek and I had been shipmates on the old wooden U.S.S. *Bear* in 1939. He was the navigator and I the sail master on that voyage of the U.S. Antarctic Service Expedition. When men sail together on expeditions they become very close, and their friendship is enduring. Many was the time I stood on the bridge with Lieutenant Dufek as he stood his watch and we talked together. Now I wrote him a letter, offering my services to go with him again.

The ball began to roll at once, because Admiral Dufek is a man of action. He took the matter up with Captain Thomas, his Chief of Staff, and the only coast guardsman connected with the expedition. My orders finally came through, instructing me as a member of the U.S. Coast Guard Reserve to report for two more years of active duty in the Coast Guard. I was to be loaned to the Navy as a technical advisor and member of the first phase of Operation Deepfreeze, 1955–57, in establishing the U.S. bases for co-operation in the International Geophysical Year of 1957–58. I would be required in Washington for the period of planning, and would then ship for the Antarctic in the fall of 1955 and lead the mechanized Reconnaissance Party for the trail-blazing establishment of Byrd Station in Marie Byrd Land. This was the region I had penetrated with Leonard Berlin and Dick Moulton in 1940, fifteen years before. But now I would be traveling with two sno-cats and a weasel for transportation instead of dog teams, and with a crew of six Seabees. After returning from the reconnaissance trip I would spend my third Antarctic night on the desolate Ross Ice Barrier, this time at Little America V.

It was up to the Task Force to safely transport to the Antarctic, and supply with all the necessary equipment and provisions, an army of especially trained men for an all-out mechanized and scientific assault upon Antarctica. Never had such a thing been attempted before.

We had to sail through the roughest of seas, penetrate the treacherous ice pack, and locate as well as construct observation sites where men could live in safety, for years if necessary, on the Antarctic continent. And why all this? Our immediate purpose, and all we needed to know about it, was that the preliminary phase, known as Operation Deepfreeze I, had been designed to facilitate U.S. scientists in recording data. But back of this was a world-wide program of international cooperation in the name and interests of science and human progress.

Our Task Force had a truly tremendous job to perform. It was a hazardous business to unload and transport hundreds of tons of supplies and heavy equipment on the ice in Antarctica. You cannot run thirty-five-ton tractors over the ice without great risk, and even the comparatively lighter weasels and snocats would be a source of hazard.

As we approached the ice pack in the U.S.S. *Glacier* in mid-December of 1955, I think we old-timers were especially conscious of a greater feeling of security brought about by the extensive equipment and the number of men. We were in a sense bringing civilization along with us. No man was alone; he was part of an army of 1,800 with a U.S. Navy fleet of ships and a Naval Air Squadron to support him. This was an "all-out assault on Antarctica."

We stood on the deck of the largest icebreaker that had ever set out to plow through the ice pack into the Ross Sea. With her 8,625-ton displacement and 310 feet length from bow to helicopter flight deck, she could forge her way through the ice in a beeline for Antarctica, where once we had butted and battered, feeling our way where open leads permitted, and where other little ships for centuries before us had been driven back, or perished.

Abreast of Scott Island we could see the outer rim of the ice pack, rising and falling gently on the calm waters, extending east and west for as far as the eye could see.

As we drew near to it, I felt that the *Glacier* herself was a little disappointed, as I was—for instead of the formidable pack of solid ice of our anticipation this was mere rubble, so broken up by the wind that any ship could go through. We worked our way south with very little difficulty, finding the ice newly frozen, and the great icebreaker plowed through it at twelve knots, an unheard-of speed for pack travel. There was little sign of pressure.

A third of the way through the pack we struck thicker ice, but there was only 6 per cent coverage with much water space. The most that the *Glacier* could do to show her mettle was to scorn the waterways. Where lesser ships would follow the open leads of water, even if they led to wide detours, she stuck to her course directly south, plowing straight through everything in her way.

We saw one big floe ahead that we thought might show what our ship was made of. She entered it at full speed, but with only six of her ten generators on the line. As she plowed her way through it, the many little ridges showed some pressure, and blocks of ice were forced up on the floe. But she came to a full stop only twice; and in each case, after backing away, it took only one run to force her way through.

The large floe cracked into many pieces from the shock as we drew to the southern edge of it. Here again we encountered thin ice, with very little snow coverage. The ship did not stop again. At 5:00 P.M. on the seventeenth of December, 1955, we broke out into the clear water of the Ross Sea after a record-breaking run of only two days. But with the dreaded South Polar pack in such a weakened condition, it could hardly be considered a good test of the qualities of this powerful ship. At no time was the ice much over ten feet thick; and at no time did we hit clear blue ice, the hardest of all. The test was yet to come.

As soon as we arrived at McMurdo Sound a party was formed and, with a weasel, sent over the bay ice toward Cape Royds, the site of Scott's old base, to look over the ice for a runway. Six planes—two Navy R5D Skymasters, the first four-engine planes ever to attempt the flight over Antarctica, two twin-engine Navy P2V Neptunes with ski wheels, and two Albatross planes—were already in New Zealand, ready to take off as scheduled for the remaining hazardous 2,400-mile leg of their historic first flight from the United States to the Antarctic. The problem was to find a runway that was smooth and where the ice was strong enough for the heavy planes to land.

The ice looked favorable as the weasel started out, and it was thought that a tractor could also make it. One was hoisted over the side, two one-ton sleds were loaded and hitched on behind, and it started off after the weasel. But neither of them got very far. The tractor became stuck in one of the many cracks and seal blowholes along the route and had to be abandoned, and the weasel went only a little further before slowly sinking through the ice and finally disappearing altogether, although fortunately not before the men escaped and some of the equipment was rescued.

The *Glacier* was still in the ice at McMurdo Sound and not on station when word was received that the planes had taken off from New Zealand. The *Edesto* came in to take up her position at McMurdo Sound as a guide to their destination.

Our convoy of seven ships, with the exception of the *Glacier* and the *Edesto,* was already strung out along the route, three hundred miles apart, to guide the planes on their flight and to be available for rescue in case of accident. So we had to drop everything, leaving a party on the ice to complete the marking of a runway, and hasten north to the *Glacier's* allotted position for the guidance of the pilots. All ten of her generators were started up and put on the line for full speed as soon as we got clear of the ice.

We had just arrived on station when the first plane flew by without our seeing it. The second changed her course a little to fly over us. It was a thrilling sight to see her winging her way on this maiden flight to the South Polar continent. The two Albatross planes failed to reach us. They were bucking a head wind all the time and had used up too much of their fuel before they had gone halfway, so they were forced to return to New Zealand. But the two big Skymasters and the two Neptunes landed safely on the ice at McMurdo Sound. We were all conscious of having witnessed the making of history that day. It was the first long-distance flight ever to be made over the southern seas to the Antarctic continent.

Before we proceeded to the Bay of Whales, some four hundred miles east of McMurdo Sound, we made a second and equally easy trip through the ice pack to pick up the rest of our convoy. As escort to these thinner-skinned ships, the mighty *Glacier* made her third passage through the pack slowly, keeping away from the ice as much as possible. Like a duck leading her ducklings, we made a way for them through one tight place after another. The helicopter made frequent reconnaissance flights ahead over the pack to ascertain the best possible track to follow.

It was a beautiful calm day, with much open water, as we sailed along by Cape Bird after completing our convoy mission.

The visibility was unlimited, and the volcano of Mount Erebus stood out against the cloudless blue sky, a plume of smoke rising from its summit into the cold air.

The water was as smooth as glass, and we made good time speeding eastward in the Ross Sea. One hundred and fifteen years before, Sir James Clark Ross sailed these waters in his frail ship and discovered the towering cliffs of the great ice barrier which now bears his name. Twenty-seven years ago I had first seen this breath-taking ice shelf from the deck of the little *City of New York*. Now we were steaming along the same Barrier in a giant icebreaker with a top speed of 19 knots, powered by diesel engines with a total output of 21,000 horsepower.

It was the maiden voyage of this mighty ship, and I felt a great pride in being with her—in having lived to see and share this day, sailing in such safety and comfort compared to earlier expeditions.

One did not have to go aloft and furl sail and take the full brunt of the icy wind. The lookout was not forced to stand in a barrel, high on the top of the fore or mainmast, as in the old days. Now he stood his wheel watch on a heated bridge, where no spray or wind could touch him, steering in comfort, and with comparative ease.

I wondered if he knew how lucky he was. On our early expeditions we stood watch on the open deck, bundled up with heavy clothes, exposed to the spray and the ice-cold winds. Before your trick at the wheel was over, you were chilled to the bone. It was no fun then; and yet it was adventure. The sails were hard as boards, the rigging coated with ice, slippery and dangerous. It was one hand for the ship and the other for yourself in those days. Now you had two hands for the ship.

It was December 28, 1955, when we stopped at the Bay of Whales. I didn't recognize the place. When I saw it for the first time, in 1928, a great bay ran in from the Barrier edge for twenty miles, and it was twelve miles wide at the mouth. When I saw it eleven years later, in 1939, the bay was five miles wide, and ran in for twelve miles instead of twenty. Now there was no sign of Floyd Bennett Bay or Lindbergh Inlet. The ice on the east side was still there, but on the west side it had broken off completely on a straight line with the bay's inner coast of the Barrier. This great slice of the ice shelf had broken off and drifted out to sea. There was just a small bay left, and it was mostly open to the Ross Sea, with very little shelter. It would never do for a base; we would have to search elsewhere.

I was shocked to realize what the years had done to the Barrier that had once been our protection. Two hundred miles of the ice shelf, a gigantic piece ten miles wide, had vanished completely. I shuddered to think of the noise it must have made, and the effect it would have had on us if we had been there. Perhaps it did not break off all in one piece; 2,000 square miles of ice is eighty times the size of Manhattan. The Bay of Whales was useless; and so were Little America I and II and III and IV. Far back on the Barrier we could see the radio poles from the fourth expedition, Operation Highjump, of 1947.

We abandoned all thought of setting up base at our old camping grounds, but broke in a half mile of ice and moored the *Glacier* in order to visit the site of our first expedition.

2

AS we went out on the flight deck of the mighty *Glacier* and got into the helicopter, I felt a strange sense of removal from Antarctica. I was here again, but something was missing that had linked me with the life of this place. It was the dogs, of course. We had tractors, planes, and helicopters, but the life and spirit of Antarctic exploration, as I knew it, had vanished.

We flew over the bay ice, edged in over the Barrier, and sank gently down alongside one of the steel radio towers we had put up in 1928 at Little America I. They had been seventy-five feet tall then. The last time I had visited them, with my dog team in 1941, not more than fifty feet were sticking up out of the snow. Now only two of the towers were visible—ten feet above the surface. The third was nowhere to be found. Our old base was more than sixty feet beneath us. I felt as if we were visiting a burial ground.

In a way it was like coming home, but with mixed feelings of pleasure and sadness. I had been a very young man in 1928. Now I had many gray hairs and was not as active as I had been in those days when I leaped over the rail of the ship to be the first man on the ice, racing and romping with my dogs.

Now those days were only memories, but vivid ones, as we

stood over the place where we had first raised the American flag and named it "Little America." I made a new flag ready, sewing the Stars and Stripes onto a bamboo pole, waiting for Admiral Byrd who was coming ashore with the last flight for the ceremony.

A few of the oldtimers were there—Lieutenant Commander Charlie Shirley, Commander Frederick Dustin, Edward Goodale—but only three of us had been present in 1928 at the first raising of the flag: Admiral Byrd, Eddie, and myself.

It was a cold, dreary day. There was no sun and the sky was a gray. A raw wind was blowing and the visibility was poor. The snow was quite soft and we sank up to our knees as we walked in it.

When Admiral Byrd arrived, he reminded me of the old times and the day I had met him when he stepped out of the *Floyd Bennett* after the polar flight. He wasn't as young now, either; we both felt the years. His hair was very white and he walked with a much slower step. But he was dressed, I thought, in the same fur suit that I used to see him wear around the base and on many of his flights. He walked over to the place I had made ready for the base of the flag pole and the ceremonies began.

"I guess I am the Mayor of this place," said the Admiral.

I raised the flag and we all saluted. It was a happy occasion, and yet I felt an undercurrent of sadness. The helicopter shuttled back and forth, taking us back on board ship. The flag was left flying. It looked awfully lonely there all by itself.

We set a course to the east along the Barrier for thirty miles until we came to Kainan Bay. Kainan Bay looked good, and it had survived the years, but before deciding on it as the base site for Little America V, Admiral Dufek sailed still further east to Okuma Bay, another Japanese discovery. Okuma Bay was large and it too looked good until we made a flight over it. We found no suitable ramp to drive tractors up on the Barrier, and there were many crevasses and cracks along the outer edge. So the Admiral decided it would not do, and we returned to Kainan Bay.

As soon as we finally settled on Kainan Bay for our new base site, things began to hum. The bay was frozen solid, and it would be a long haul for the tractors over the ice to a place on the Barrier safe enough for the base. So it was decided to give the *Glacier* a chance to show her icebreaking qualities.

All ten of her generators were immediately put on the line, and with Captain Maher on the bridge she backed off into the clear water for her first run. He pushed the controls ahead for full power, which checked her sternway. Then she began to forge ahead, gaining speed as she approached the ice. She struck it with a terriffic blow that shook her from stem to stern. Trembling and rolling, she began to rise, climbing up on the solid mass to break it down by sheer weight.

This was heavy ice, ten to fifteen feet thick, that had been freezing all winter. It required immense power to penetrate it. Ice splinters flew in all directions as she plowed her way into it by a length and a half of her 310 feet.

Still, this was nothing. A tremendous bight had to be broken into the frozen bay to make a harbor where three large ships could tie up with safety. There was a crack a mile farther in which was Captain Maher's objective. Clearing a large Antarctic bay of solid ice had never been done before, and the Captain had to conceive a technique for going about it.

I had admired Captain Maher's skill before, and had observed his know-how in piloting icebreakers through heavy ice. I was navigating officer on the C.G.C. *Northwind* when he was skipper of the *Burton Island,* our companion ship in the Bering

Sea, and I had worked side by side with him. I knew that if any man understood his job, he did.

The Captain backed her off time and again, making cuts square into the solid ice. After she had traveled half her length into the mass, he would give right or left rudder, thus causing the ice to split. He was breaking out the bay in a semicircle, maneuvering the *Glacier* like an ax blade being driven into a log. And with the wind blowing off the ice, the broken pieces drifted out of the bight which he enlarged at every run.

All that night he kept at it, assigning other officers to relieve him in order to give them some experience. By morning a great bay had been cleared, and the powerful icebreaker delivered her men to a safe berth at Little America V, triumphant. Two cargo ships, the *Arneb* and the *Greenville Victory*, tied up behind her. Then the unloading began.

It was a perfect day and the sun was shining warmly as the men from the ships visited back and forth before settling down to the tough job ahead of them. Men bragged about the weather and said the Antarctic wasn't as cold as the other expeditions had reported it. I admitted that it was unusually warm, no worse than winter at home; but, after all, it was summer in Antarctica, and day or night the sun never set during its four months. They would soon find out how cold it could get.

When I saw the hundreds of tons of supplies and equipment that had to be hoisted out and hauled over the ice, I realized both the boon and necessity of machinery on this expedition. How we had toiled, sweated, and pulled with our faithful dogs on previous expeditions to move five hundred tons many miles over the ice and snow at Little America! But five hundred tons included the whole expedition, and that was but a drop in the bucket compared to what faced the men now. Thirty-five-ton tractors would do the work, carrying tons on big trailers, traveling at a speed of three miles per hour. The men would drive in heated cabs, with their coats off and wearing no mittens. With the dogs, we had bucked winds that cut our faces like a knife. Our lips chapped and bled and our eyes were blinded from the glare of the sun on the ice. We always had to carry our sleeping bags in case we were caught in a blizzard, unable to find our way to the base.

But for all that, I would not trade my memories with these Construction Drivers. With all their hardships, those early days were Adventure, men and dogs against the ice; this was organized and mechanized attack, the systematic invasion of a hostile environment.

A dump of supplies was started two miles in, on the ice near the ramp that went up to the Barrier. Tractors plied back and forth from the ship to the dump with businesslike regularity, hauling heavy loads and going back for more. At the dump the loads were separated and marked with flags to identify them.

Meanwhile, a party of us left the ships to pick a trail over the ice and find a site for Little America V. We traveled on skis for seven miles before we found a place on top of the Barrier that seemed safe and suitable; and there we laid our base.

Day and night the tractors shuttled back and forth as the piles of freight grew at the dumping site. Then on New Year's Day the men were given a holiday, and a beer party was held alongside the ships. "We're here because we're here because we're here because we're here," the men chanted.

The comparatively warm weather, unusual for the Antarctic, persisted, with temperatures rising slightly above freezing. This made it easier for the men working outdoors, but it brought on a crisis. A surveyor noticed the ice edge heaving up and down out in the bay. Admiral Dufek ordered everything moved from the dump to the base site within forty-eight hours. A blizzard blew down on us, and all hands fought around the clock as the edge of the ice started breaking up into a heaving turmoil. The last load of supplies was not long off the bay ice when the rising seas and wind broke up the ice altogether and swept it out into the Ross Sea. The ships moved in and tied up to the face of the Barrier, which came up only to deck level here.

We had lost no supplies and had had no casualties in Kainan Bay, but the ice claimed its first human victim over at McMurdo Sound. Construction Driver Richard T. Williams drove a thirty-five-ton D8 tractor over a bridged crack in the bay ice. He got over it, but suddenly the ice split in all directions and the tractor went down as Williams tried to get out of the door. He never did. He went down with his vehicle into a hundred fathoms of water.

As soon as my crew of Seabees and I could lay our hands on our equipment at the base site of Little America V, we went to work on it. To do this we moved from the ship to the base site with all our gear. None of the huts had been completed, so we put up tents and began to live as if we already were on the trail.

We had eight one-ton sleds and two dog-type sleds that I had made and hand-lashed while still in the United States. These were flexible and would follow the curvature of the snow. They would be towed by the weasel, breaking trail for the two sno-cats each hauling four of the heavier sleds. We had to assemble and load everything that would be necessary to support and maintain seven men and three vehicles for sixty days over a distance of six hundred miles and back.

I had figured on man-pemmican for the main food ration, with just a few delicacies to offset the monotony of the diet. That had been our mainstay on every previous trip into the interior of Antarctica. But during our stay at McMurdo Sound it was universally reported by the men that the pemmican tasted terrible and could not be eaten.

I insisted that the pemmican was good, and to support my argument I cooked some of it, making it into a mush. From experience, I knew that a hungry man out on the trail would learn to relish it. But I admit that I showed a little more gusto to establish my point than my palate felt in eating it. The boys, however, held their noses and called me "Pemmican Jack."

"You can have it," they said. "We want no part of it."

So we devised a new plan for food. Stevens and Levesque broke open the trail ration boxes and substituted other balanced food for the pemmican. Only one package of pemmican was included. This, the boys claimed, was to be my food alone.

When I looked over the rations selected, I was astonished. I found steaks, eggs, hams, oatmeal, bacon, beans, ninety loaves of bread, all kinds of fruit juices, peaches, pears, apricots, and other delicacies. And there was cocoa as well as tea and coffee for our hot drinks.

This was all real luxury, so far as I was concerned, and unheard of in all the annals of polar traveling. And it was a diet that loaded one sled which could otherwise have taken seven drums of gasoline. My polar conscience winced considerably.

After all, it was argued, this was the most modern of all expeditions; I was old-fashioned. Our mode of travel was far superior to the days of dog and teams, and we could haul a much heavier load. Also, we would travel faster, and our days in the field would be reduced to one-third . . . if nothing happened to the vehicles. That possibility was always with us.

3

WEDEMEYER, my mechanic, had put in long hours getting the spare parts ready, going over the machines and testing them to be sure they were in tiptop shape. I had great faith in him, and when he informed me that they were as good as he could make them, I knew that we were all set to move.

The sky was overcast and I could not see the sun as I looked down and out over Kainan Bay from the tent at the base site on the morning of our departure. A helicopter was rising from the deck of the U.S.S. *Arneb* at the edge of the Barrier, tilting into the raw wind that was blowing from the east. I knew it was bringing Captain Thomas and Commander Whitney to see us off.

Bud Waite, a veteran of past expeditions, was there in his weasel from the Army Signal Corps. Bob Haun, a commercial artist assigned to Operation Deepfreeze I, was also on hand. Cameras were clicking. Men talked in little groups. A D8 tractor came out with a drum of gasoline on a one-ton sled to top off our tanks. Then came the pat on the back, the last handshake. I gave the order and we were off.

Waite followed us in the Signal Corps weasel for a little way, taking pictures of the train, and then he left us. A few miles out the helicopter flew over us as a last farewell. Then we were traveling alone, heading into this great open space of snow and ice on an easterly course.

Our assignment was to blaze a safe trail over the Barrier and the Rockefeller Plateau to a position some six hundred miles inland where we would select a site in Marie Byrd Land for a base to be called Byrd Station.

On the second day we had stopped to lay down our first fifty-mile cache. Everyone pitched in at shoveling snow to build the snow beacon, while I sewed an orange flag on the ten-foot bamboo pole we carried on the sled for marking. By the time I had the bunting sewed fast to the pole, the beacon was ready and I stuck it in place. We left a drumful of gas and part of another to fill our tanks on the way back.

Would we come back? I thought of the many crevasses I had crossed before, on skis behind a dog team, often saving my neck by a hair's-breadth from an icy tomb hundreds of feet below.

I tried to forget these pictures, but I knew that, even though I might blaze a trail to the proposed inland position, I would never be able truthfully to say or feel that I had blazed a trail that would be safe and sure for heavy tractors to follow. For no man, regardless of his experience, can tell the thickness of the bridges that cover hidden abysses many fathoms below. No man can estimate the strength of the bridge of ice and snow, or the weight that it will hold for a safe crossing.

I was riding on the sled back of the tractorlike weasel where I could see the surface better. Big Ed was driving the weasel, breaking the trail. Every quarter mile he stopped so I could plant one of the International orange flags to mark the trail. Big Ed, as we called A. G. Edwards, was a Construction Driver of the U.S. Naval Construction Battalion Special; one of the crew of six Seabees who had been assigned to the Reconnaissance Party under my leadership.

Every time I planted a flag I glanced back to align it and to see if our two sno-cats, each hauling four one-ton sleds behind them, were following safely. Levesque, another Construction Driver, was driving one of them; and George Moss, our navigator, was driving the other. The remaining three of our crew were riding in the cabs of the vehicles: C. M. Stevens, our photographer; R. J. Dube, our radioman; and C. H. Wedemeyer, our mechanic, ever alert to respond to emergency.

I am sure the rest of the boys felt safer than I did, because we were on the solid Barrier. We were three days out, and the surface was good. The vehicles were working well and we were making good time. We had encountered no crevasses, and at the speed we were traveling, it appeared as if we would be on the Rockefeller Plateau in a short time. We could see it already. But I was more keenly aware of the difficulties. Dick Moulton, Leonard Berlin, and I had traveled more than six hundred miles in this direction sixteen years before and had crossed numerous crevassed areas with dog teams.

Crevasses have always been the main obstacles in traveling over the great ice Barrier, and every man who has ever sledged over them knows the dangers involved. That is why a wave of warning went up my spine as I rode the sled back to the weasel, when we ran over a little ridge that slightly jarred me. We were only four or five miles from the plateau itself, but my hopes of reaching it were shattered when we crossed a second ridge immediately after the first one. This spelled real danger.

I motioned Big Ed to stop, and the sno-cats stopped with us. I skied ahead a short distance and came to an ugly-looking hole in the Barrier. We blew it open with a charge of dynamite and found that it dropped down seventy feet into inky blackness, forming a belly large enough to swallow a block-house and all of our vehicles. I went on ahead for a quarter of a mile, until I was surrounded by hundreds of crevasses. The prospect all around me was appalling. The area we were in was nothing but a mass of crumbling ice, with jagged tongues jutting out from the plateau, spelling danger on all sides.

The treacherous patterns ran north and south for as far as I could see. All my plans for ascending the plateau collapsed in the face of this situation; it was impossible to go on. But we were less than eighty miles of the proposed goal of six hundred, so we could not stop here. To fill the crevasses and form bridges over them would take years, even though the area was only three or four miles wide. There wasn't room to maneuver the tractors between the broken-up ice and snow. And even if we should succeed in picking a way through this area with the weasel and sno-cats, the heavy tractors could never make it.

Our progress completely blocked, I called for my support plane so I could view the treacherous area from the air before deciding what to do about it.

The UC-1 was soon seen heading toward us, flying low over the Barrier; it landed between the lines of flags I had placed for it. Lloyd Beebe from the Disney Studios had come along as a passenger, bringing his camera. We wasted little time in con-versation. Beebe stayed at camp and Moss and I got in for the reconnaissance flight. I told Lieutenant Commander Lathrop, the pilot, and Lieutenant Streich, his copilot, that I wanted to fly along the face of the plateau to find, if possible, a ramp with a safe route to it that could be used by the tractors.

The visibility was perfect and there was not a cloud in the direction of our flight. The plateau stood out like a bold white monster along the horizon, beautiful to look at. As soon as we gained altitude, I could see the Rockefeller Mountains in the distance. But we flew back and forth for many miles over thousands of crevasses and saw no sign of a ramp by which we could gain the plateau, even if there had been a safe route to it.

The safe and solid surface of the plateau we sought to reach glistened like a silver platter shining in the sun; but a hundred miles of treacherous terrain, three miles wide, blocked our way to it. I was astonished at the great change which had come over the place during the fifteen years since I had last traversed this area. The Barrier then had been smooth at this longitude, showing very little sign of crevasses, and we had traveled over it on skis with dog teams and had had little difficulty ascending the plateau. I remembered, too, my first sight of it in 1929 when a few of us went up in the Fokker plane with Bernt Balchen. That was when I first sensed the immensity of this mighty continent.

Now a great upheaval had apparently taken place at the dividing line where plateau meets Barrier. What caused this terrific disturbance in millions of tons of solid ice I cannot say. Perhaps the whole Barrier was getting ready to move north into the open sea, and this was the first split of the mass of ice that connects the floating ice shelf with the continental plateau.

As I looked down upon the scene from the air I could see no way in which we could safely proceed to the plateau in heavy vehicles. Yet we had to do it; it was unthinkable to stop at seventy-eight miles, more than five hundred miles short of our goal.

We returned to camp, deciding to try again the next day. Lathrop, Streich, and Beebe returned to the base in the plane and the rest of us settled down for a "night" in the midnight sun. Stevens spent much time and effort preparing a steak dinner on three primus stoves that did not work very well. All seven of us crowded into the tent to eat and talk over our situation.

Our method of camping was to run the vehicles up side by side, leaving space between the sno-cats for pitching our tent. The tent guy-lines were tied to the tracks of the vehicles instead of to metal pegs driven into the snow. This worked pretty well, and saved much time whenever we stopped to sleep. Two men slept in the tent and two in each of the sno-cats. I slept in the weasel.

Before we left the United States, the cab of the weasel had been extended at the right-hand side thirty-four inches to facilitate the use of a bunk. A standard spring bunk frame was put in and a hole cut in the stern for the storage of gear.

The bunk was comfortable to sleep in, but the space allowed for getting in and out was small. I found that only a contortionist could crawl in and out of a sleeping bag with so little room above it.

At 6:30 A.M. I called the boys because the day was such a perfect one. I decided to backtrack and swing north while waiting for the plane, thinking that we might find a way around or through the crevasse area in that direction.

After breaking camp and getting under way, we backtracked ten miles and then changed our course to the north of east. Dube kept his radio schedule and we dispatched a message to the pilots of the Otter, telling them how to find us and giving them weather reports.

We had gone only seven miles on the new course before we struck crevasses again. We blew one open, but only a small hole showed up so we considered it safe to cross over it.

This crevasse gave me a warning of danger, however, so I put on my skis and went ahead of the vehicles. I came to a wide crevasse, but it seemed to be bridged very strongly. We had the crevasse detector fastened to the weasel, but the readings on the dial went haywire, and we could not depend on it.

It was very crudely built in the first place and soon fell apart.

We made another mile without mishap and then got into a place that looked truly ugly. So rather than move around the unseen holes, I decided to camp right there and wait for the plane again.

In our radio schedule with the base I was told that due to the closed-in conditions at Little America Station, the plane would not fly that day. Here at our camp the visibility was unlimited and there was not a cloud in the sky. We were about thirty miles from the Rockefeller Mountains, which were standing out as plainly as the Statue of Liberty on a clear day.

However, there was nothing I could do about it, so I let the boys rest and sleep-in the next morning, although I hated to see another beautiful morning go by without a reconnaissance flight. I prepared for the plane by marking out a runway with flags between two large crevasses that ran parallel to each other.

At noon the plane found us, and Lieutenant Streich made a wonderful landing between the crevasses. In the afternoon we made a two-hour reconnaissance flight, covering the whole Barrier in this section from Okuma Bay east to the Rockefellers, then onto the plateau and south along its face. Here we made repeated runs east and west, trying to spot a safe route.

If we found a route, we planned to mark a trail with flags by plane, if possible. We dropped a flag to see whether it would stick in the snow right end up and then circled to investigate the result of our experiment. The flag was standing straight up, so we flew low over the surface looking for a route that might be marked in this way.

The weather favored us; it was so clear that we could see every ridge and crevasse on the Barrier. In one place, flying west from the plateau, we saw a route that was partly clear, with only a few crevasses visible from the air. We returned to the vehicles and planned to mark the trail from the air next day. For this purpose the plane stayed with us overnight. The two pilots slept in a small survival tent that they carried with them, while the mechanic slept in our larger tent with two of my men.

When we awoke, however, the sky was overcast, gray and forbidding. The visibility was poor. The plane could not fly, so we were idle for the whole day.

The next morning the visibility was good as I rolled from my bunk in the weasel. The sun was shining brilliantly and it was perfect flying weather. I could see every ridge in the Barrier clearly.

Everyone was feeling good as we ate our breakfast. Lieutenant Commander Lathrop, Lieutenant Streich, and their mechanic proceeded to make the plane ready for the take-off on our attempt at aerial trail-blazing. The door of the plane was taken off and we put on board three hundred flags to be dropped at equal intervals when a final choice of route had been made.

I sent my navigator, Moss, and the photographer, Stevens, on the flight to establish the route and remained behind to break camp and backtrack our vehicles out of the crevasse area.

We wormed our way out, and once clear of the crevasses we followed our trail back to the main line again, where we had agreed to meet the plane. We had backtracked another ten miles, however, before we sighted the plane coming east over the trail and dropping low for a landing.

As soon as Moss and Stevens had stepped out, the door was attached again and the plane took off for Little America V. Lathrop and Streich had done a splendid job of completing a trail run of one hundred miles, dropping flags along the way at twenty-second intervals. The rest was up to us.

The visibility was holding good, and we had little difficulty in following the new trail by sighting the flags that had been dropped from the plane. We marked the route, however, by planting flags at more frequent intervals.

The midnight sun enabled us to keep on going through the "night." We were now making better time than we had anticipated, and had not yet struck any crevasses when we stopped to build Cache No. 2 at a point one hundred miles from Little America Station. We had traveled fifty miles without stopping, and with our heavy loads on ten sleds this was something I would not have believed possible fifteen years before.

We were tired after traveling all day and far into the night, but after making Cache No. 2 the boys agreed to go on because visibility was so perfect. We stopped only long enough to warm up a pot of coffee, although we had had nothing to eat except chocolate bars that we carried in our pockets. For drink on the trail Stevens issued orange, pineapple, or tomato juice to each vehicle every morning. It was always frozen, but we thawed it out by setting the can down on the floor of the sno-cat or weasel. Here it gradually melted enough so that by punching two holes in the top of the can we could suck out the juice.

The route we were following made a gradual turn, veering toward the south and drawing closer to the Rockefeller Mountains. After another five miles I decided we had better have a hot meal and sleep a few hours before we hit any crevasses. We set up camp and ate, then crawled into our sleeping bags. My last thought was to pray for the weather to hold out. Even a fog or a white-out would turn trail work into a game of blindman's-buff; and a blizzard was bad enough anywhere in Antarctica, but deadly in a crevasse area.

We cut our sleep short and broke camp again the same afternoon at 3:00 P.M. Continuing visibility was a good omen for ascending the plateau, if we could make it.

We came now to the section of the crevasse area which had looked the least hazardous when we viewed it from the air. Even from a close surface inspection none of the crevasses we encountered here looked as bad as the ones we had previously been up against. They were not very wide, and looking down in them we could see a firm wall on each side. Our vehicles crossed them without difficulty, but for the thirty-five-ton tractors of the tractor train that would follow us, the men would have to bulldoze snow into some of the crevasses and fill them up to make a more solid bridge. Little did we think that one of these crevasses which we had safely crossed ourselves would later swallow a D8 tractor and its driver seventy-five feet deep, both to stay there until the end of time.

To right and left of us we could see the indentations of crevasses running north and south, and it was evident from the surface as it had been from the air that we had found the one feasible route through the area.

As we neared the plateau, we were ascending a rise with a crevasse directly ahead of us which I thought it best to detour. We could see no more flags, so I was leading the vehicles on skis, looking for a good ramp that would take us up the incline to the plateau. When I found one, I waved my ski pole for the vehicles to follow me, anxious to get up on the broad plain while the visibility was still good.

We stopped the weasel on the edge of the plateau for Dube to keep his radio schedule, and I reported our safe arrival and said we could breathe easy at last, for the treacherous crevasses were behind us.

The surface on the plateau proved to be rougher than that of the Barrier. It was ridged with sastrugi, causing our vehicles to roll and toss violently, and almost dislocating our backbones. Riding on the crest of one of these ice ridges, the weasel would suddenly fall over into the trough. It was at times as if some unseen hand yanked our bodies to a sudden stop in one direction and then drove them at terrific speed in the opposite direction, with a jolt that jarred every bone and organ.

We had to travel slowly for fear of breaking a track, ripping the transmission and tearing the whole machine to pieces. The knifelike ice ridges cut across our trail in a confusion of directions. We ran in third and fourth gear most of the time to save the machines as much as possible. This was no place for a hot-rod driver; but slowly as we went, we could not relax or drive carelessly. We kept our eyes glued to the surface of the snow in order to ease the machines over the wicked-looking surface.

By the time our meters indicated we were two hundred of the proposed six hundred miles from Little America V, we were all exhausted from the pounding and our bodies ached. Every fifty miles we laid down a cache, and considered that we were doing all right if we made that distance in a day of ten hours. But as we neared the 300-mile mark, a low-lying mist set in and the next morning there was no horizon as we started up the vehicles. The whiteness had drawn a circle around us, closing down visibility to less than one hundred feet. Proceeding cautiously, we made thirty miles over comparatively smooth surface and then struck more crevasses. We turned our vehicles around and re-traced our tracks for a mile to a safe area. The white-out gripped us from all sides and above. We could see nothing and could hear nothing except the sound of a trail flag flapping in the wind close by.

The only thing we could do was stay right where we were until we could see again; so we set up camp and crawled into our sleeping bags.

Around midnight I opened my eyes, thinking I heard a plane in the distance. I lay there wondering what it could be, because no plane could find us in this enclosure of mist, or even attempt to do so. But I heard it again and struggled out of my sleeping bag with emergency action in mind: to send up flares, get Dube busy on the radio, make smoke—anything to help the pilot if it should really be the Otter, our support plane. We were only one little dot on an endless mass of ice buried in mist. There were no landmarks visible to a pilot, no trail to follow, nothing to guide him; how could he ever hope to find us?

Just then Big Ed stuck his head in the door of the weasel and cried, "The plane!"

I glanced in a southerly direction and caught a faint glimpse of wings flying through the scud above us.

"There she is!" I yelled.

But I could barely see her as she banked to come in for a landing.

I couldn't comprehend how Lieutenant Commander Lathrop had found us, even after he told us his story; for it was then that we realized the great risk he had taken. He had flown over three hundred miles without seeing a thing but the white void in which he was flying. He crisscrossed our trail many times without seeing it. His gas was getting low and his dead reckoning could not be relied on because of the many times he had changed his course. The good hand of Providence must have been guiding him, for it was only by chance that Mechanic Brown AD2 happened to look down through a small break in the blinding mist and catch a glimpse of us. Lathrop and Streich had done a magnificent job of piloting. Also, they had brought me two drums of gasoline, which was good news because we were beginning to run low and had only enough for another hundred miles.

The plane and its crew stayed with us until the weather lifted and we found a route to get around the crevasse area safely. Shortly after we left Cache No. 7 we broke out into beautiful weather again. The pure, cold air was cutting my face and frost was freezing on my whiskers, but my body was warm as I scanned the way ahead for any sign of danger. I was standing on the floor of the weasel with my head up through the hatch in the top. This was my observation post when the weather and visibility permitted it.

We had just received a message from Admiral Dufek congratulating us on the progress we were making. It was a stimulant for us all. This was our day. Everything was clear ahead. The going was better and we were sailing along at 10 knots on a straight course, stopping only to plant flags. Then suddenly smoke began to come from the weasel, and thinking it was on fire, Ed stopped immediately. Wedemeyer found that a hole had burnt in the water hose and we had to make repairs.

Again we went on, and then I saw ahead of us the very thing I had most dreaded: another large area of crevasses. It was a truly big one this time. The turmoil of twisted ice stretched out its knifelike edges for as far as I could see. To the north, east, and south were long lines of rolling domes and heaved-up tangles of broken pressure such as I had seen and encountered on the first expedition in what Amundsen had called "The Trap."

We were now 381 miles on a straight line from Little America V, but we had traveled 460 miles as registered by the vehicles on the trail. Our loads were lighter, and if we could find our way around this crevasse area, we would have only 100 to 150 miles to go to reach our goal at Longitude 120° West. We were now at Longitude 134° West, with 14 degrees to go. Our objective for laying Byrd Station was 80° South, 10 degrees from the Pole, on the 120th meridian.

Dube kept his radio schedule with the base and called for the plane. While we were waiting for it, we turned in for a sleep.

4

WHEN the plane didn't arrive, Dube radioed again and was informed it was in the air. But we could neither see nor hear any sign of it.

After waiting some time longer, Dube tried to make direct contact with the Otter, but got no answer. The base could not raise her, either. Finally we received word that the plane had landed again at Little America. After seven hours of flying the pilots could not find us, so had returned to the base with only a few gallons of gas left in the tanks. This was on the first day of February.

Then I received a message from Commander Whitney that approximately four hundred miles would be satisfactory for Byrd Station. The plane would fly us back and we were to leave the vehicles. Commander Whitney's order disappointed me, but we had to abide by it. I felt that a reconnaissance flight would have revealed a way around this new bad area of crevasses, and that we could have gone on the full six hundred miles. But "orders are orders" and I began to plan the station immediately. We figured the best approach for setting it up, the way to protect the machines we would leave, the mode of storing food and equipment. All this was for naught, but we did not then know that it would be decided eventually to push on to the goal originally intended. However, our reconnaissance trip, with its worst of the trail blazing, was over.

When we finally sighted the plane flying in low over the trail toward us, we shot flares up into the air to welcome them.

"Well, boys," I said to my crew of Seabees, "this is our big day."

Besides Lieutenant Commander Lathrop, Lieutenant Streich, and Airplane Crew Chief Floyd, Lloyd Beebe of the Disney Studios had come along to get moving pictures of this finale to our reconnaissance trip. That made eight of us besides the plane crew. I knew that with our personal gear we could not all go on in one flight.

So I asked Lieutenant Commander Lathrop, "How many men do you intend to take on the first flight?"

"Four men," he replied, "with all their baggage."

That was when I felt a premonition. I can't explain it, but I was influenced by a sudden feeling that something might happen and that we might have to drive the vehicles all the way back instead of leaving them there. This governed my choice of men to remain with me for the second flight. With the mechanic for repairs and our radioman to maintain contact with the base, there would be three of us to drive the weasel and the two sno-cats. Lloyd Beebe could come along with us as a passenger. So I told Chief Moss, Edwards, Levesque, and Stevens to get ready for the first trip.

After we had taken the official pictures of the beacon, with the American flag flying atop it on a bamboo pole, we loaded the equipment into the plane. As the men climbed on board, Lathrop called over his shoulder, "I'll be back for you within six hours, Jack."

This would give us plenty of time to get the equipment in

place and ready the station for our departure. We watched the plane until it was airborne and out of sight, then went to work.

The hours passed and the plane had not returned, nor had it arrived at Little America. Dube tried to call the plane, but got no response. He called the base and was informed that they too had been unable to contact the plane. There was nothing but silence.

When seven hours had gone by, we knew that the plane must be down. It shocked me to think that my premonition had been justified. Now I knew we would have to drive the vehicles back, so while awaiting instructions I began making preparations.

I had nothing to go on from my end of the trail. I did not know what course the plane had flown, but felt pretty sure that they did not try to follow the trail back. My concern was: How could we aid them? There was no other plane at Little America. They would have to wait until one was flown from McMurdo Sound, or brought to Kainan Bay by ship if the weather prevented flying the four hundred miles. We were still another four hundred miles east, and there was no telling where the Otter was, or in what condition the men were. Assuming they were uninjured, we figured they had only seven days' food, at the most, for six men; and without a rescue plane, without even dogs at the base, their situation could be desperate.

When the orders came to follow the trail back in the vehicles and keep a good lookout, we lost no time getting started. My orders were to establish a temporary base at Cache No. 4 for the operation of a plane already on its way from McMurdo Sound aboard the C.G.C. *Eastwind*. All efforts to make it by air had failed. The area between McMurdo Sound and Kainan Bay was completely blanked out in the zero visibility of a white-out.

As well as an Otter, Admiral Dufek was bringing a helicopter with him on the *Eastwind*. He had ordered two Sky-

masters and an Albatross to stand by at the New Zealand
Wigram Air Force Base in case they were needed. The crew of
a long-range U.S. Navy patrol bomber volunteered to set forth
from the Naval Air Base at Patuxent, Maryland. This two-engine
Neptune P2V was bringing a Marine parachutist in case the
missing plane was found in a region otherwise inaccessible. No
efforts were being spared to save the lives of our men, if any of
them should still be surviving.

We learned later that the Neptune P2V was downed in a
jungle in Venezuela while on their way to us, but the men on
board were uninjured and were soon found by search planes.

Meanwhile, a base search party in two weasels had met us,
after traveling all night on the trail we had blazed. Between
us, we had completely covered the trail route from Little America
V to the end of our trail, nearly four hundred miles east—the
point from which the missing plane had last taken off. There
had been no sign of the plane or the men within sight of the
trail. We set up camp with the base search party, as we all
needed some sleep.

While I was pondering the probable fate of the plane party,
I saw something that both pleased and disturbed me. A little
Antarctic petrel, beautiful in its snowy white feathers with black
claws and beak, paid us a visit. He sat on the snow close by the
vehicles and seemed glad of our company. He was the only
sign of life in this desolate area. But he had been blown a long
way from his nesting place and his companions. I wondered how
far the plane had been blown off its course in the same direction.
If this was any indication, they might be up in the mountains,
in which case there was no way we could help them with surface
vehicles; it was a job for the Naval Air Squadron.

The next day we broke camp and drove to Cache No. 4,
where we set up a base for the arrival of the rescue plane. It was

a beautiful day, at last, and the visibility was unlimited; but we could see no sign of life within the circle of our local horizon.

A day later we received word by radio that an Otter had arrived at Little America and was making search flights, but as yet had sighted nothing and had been unable to make any radio contact. Our party had disappeared on the third of February, and this was the seventh.

On the evening of the eighth, word was flashed that the missing Otter plane was sighted in the Alexander Mountains where it had crashed, but that it was impossible for the rescue plane to land there. When the helicopter reached the location with a doctor a few hours later, it was found that the plane had been abandoned. The helicopter crew followed the tracks of the men for more than ten miles, through a bad crevasse area toward the Rockefeller Mountains, then lost the trail.

Hours later, on the ninth, the men were sighted forty-five miles from the scene of the crash, still eighty miles from base. On foot, and with Moss and Edwards pulling a 300-pound sled, they had averaged fifteen miles per day, trudging each day for ten hours and then camping in a tent made of parachutes. Before starting, they had camped for four days by the plane after it had nosed into a mountainside when the wings iced up. Aside from face lacerations suffered by Lieutenant Streich, none of the men had been seriously injured.

When we were informed that our men had been safely brought in to Little America by helicopter, we were still at Cache No. 4. We finally arrived at the base after having been on the trail twenty-seven days and covering a round-trip distance of 920 miles. By comparison with 83 days for 1,220 miles on skis with dog teams in 1940, the advantage of mechanized transport and trail-blazing is at once apparent. But there was a price to pay for it.

After we returned to the base, Chief Machinist Young led a tractor train part way out on our trail to establish a fuel cache for the following spring. It would be a long haul to Byrd Station for heavy machines traveling two miles per hour; and without a fuel cache they could not possibly make it.

When the tractor party was 110 miles out from Little America V, they came to our route through the crevasse area at the edge of the Rockefeller Plateau, and to the few crevasses we had crossed twice in our sno-cats and weasel. They blew open the first one with dynamite and used a bulldozer to fill it with snow. Max Kiel, a young Construction Driver, drove over it twice in one of the heavy tractors. When he was backing up the third time, the crevasse in back of him caved in and the tractor fell seventy-five feet, wedging itself between the narrow walls below. Kiel was killed instantly and could not be extricated, nor could the tractor be recovered.

Two weasels were dispatched from the base with the chaplain, who conducted burial services over the crevasse where Kiel lay. This incident cast a gloom over the whole camp, because in the isolation of our little community we felt very close to one another. Morale was low, anyway; I noticed it soon after our return from the reconnaissance trip. When morale takes a drop in a group of men something has to be done about it. Associated Press correspondent Saul Pett had broken the first drop in morale on the expedition by saying, "Let's go out on the ice and build snowwomen."

But as the time approached for seventy-two of us to be marooned on that desolate shelf of ice for the long Antarctic night, the men all felt the sense of danger that is so imminent here. From the entering of the ice pack until the very day of leaving it again, it stalks every step. But the mysteries of this unknown land will be known only by the men who risk their lives to open up its secrets. This mighty continent is difficult to penetrate, and there could be little doubt that more lives would be lost before it would be conquered by man. The heavy mechanical equipment of modern exploration added more to the human risk and increased the dangers of the Antarctic. When we used dog teams, we had many narrow escapes and many dogs died for man; but we all came home alive.

I missed the dogs which had been so much a part of my life on previous expeditions and in all my experience with snow and ice since boyhood in Newfoundland. Now the nearest dogs were more than four hundred miles away at McMurdo Sound, where thirty were kept for rescue purposes. We needed a dog at Little America V for a mascot and morale booster. So when the *Glacier* came from McMurdo Sound for her final visit and to take our last mail out, she brought us one.

When a tractor shuttled up from the *Glacier* to the base with the dog in a crate, everyone felt good about it. When he was carried into the tunnel, crate and all, a happy feeling spread through the camp. The morale of every man at Little America V was raised. Now we had a dog to pet and fondle and play with, and every man had his turn at it as we took him out of the crate and tried to make him feel at home. The boys even fed him a steak; the best was none too good for him.

But for a lonely dog, a gang of men could not replace his own kind or a single master. It was not long before he got out of his crate and ran out of the tunnel into a blizzard. Every man working around the camp kept a close watch, but there was no sign of him. When the blizzard cleared, we looked for tracks, but they had been obliterated. The weather was not good enough for a search by helicopter, so we had to give him up. Every man in camp felt sorry about it; but no one felt any sorrier than I.

5

THE *Glacier* was the last ship to go, leaving seventy-two of us on the barren ice shelf at Kainan Bay out of more than 1,800 men who had invaded this loneliest spot on earth. Over at Hut Point on McMurdo Sound there were ninety men. We were the voluntary American "outcasts" who had submitted themselves to endure the long Antarctic night. We were obliged to wait for the sun to come back again in order to complete the 1957 base-laying preparations for the International Geophysical Year.

Not many words were spoken as we stood waving our last farewell to the crew and men aboard the great icebreaker. She had been our fortress of safety, and she was our last link with home and civilization.

I felt more alone, I think, than any of the rest of the boys. They were all new, and did not fully realize what lay ahead; it would be their first experience of an Antarctic night. After 5,760 hours of freezing darkness and howling blizzards on the Barrier, on my past expeditions, I knew what was ahead.

As the *Glacier* pulled out on the tenth of March in 1956, the ghosts of all the little ships of earlier days went with her in my memory. I lived every previous hour of parting again, and the ghosts of my dogs stood beside me.

We worked seven days a week to get things in shape before the blizzards would cover our supplies and equipment scattered around the encampment. There still were buildings to go up, and the 1,000-foot tunnel was only partly completed. The snow began to pile up as we worked, and much digging had to be done. It was getting darker each day as the nights lengthened, and intense cold began to grip the icy continent. There was no complaining at the amount of work, because everyone realized how vital it was to have the necessary things under cover. There could be no let-up until the base was established and in complete readiness for the long months of darkness.

The buildings went up fast. Once the footing was down and squared, it was only a matter of sorting out the right pieces and putting them together. After the floor was laid down, the walls and roof followed. There were no nails driven, as on earlier expeditions, for the panels were put together with metal clips that were then hammered in. This saved time, but even so, it was a cold job with snow blowing in our faces. It was always miserable and often almost unbearable.

The moment a building was completed, a portable heater was set up until a central heating system could be installed.

The galley was one of the first considerations because it was vital for the men to have hot meals as well as coffee at all times. The heat was also a great comfort during working hours, as the men could step inside for a few minutes to warm up.

Instead of digging tunnels and roofing them over, as we had done on previous expeditions, our 1,000-foot Main Street tunnel was built up on the surface with two-by-fours covered over with chicken wire and burlap. The snow would soon drift over this, and we would have a tunnel without digging it.

The most needed, and the most hated, tool of our earlier Antarctic base had been the shovel. We worked like demons with it to get things squared away for the winter before a blizzard came down on us and our tunnels filled up again.

That was one of the lessons of the Antarctic night in those days. Again and again you shoveled a path or a tunnel, and when you woke up, after going to bed exhausted, you started in all over again. You learned not to get mad about it—or you would go mad. You just laughed, and started to dig again.

Working out of doors with a shovel on those early expeditions was a punishing job. Now there were tractors and bulldozers to help with this. But out-of-door work on machinery had a brutality all its own. Many times CWO George Purinton and his force of mechanics had to work with bare hands to change spark plugs, clean carburetors, and make other repairs on the vehicles. The cold iron felt to fingers like a red-hot stove. The fingers stuck to the metal, and when they were pulled off, skin was left hanging.

To build and operate the base, the tractors had to be kept running day and night to complete the job. Snow had to be plowed again and again around the base to keep it from piling up, and huge snowdrifts had to be broken down by bulldozing. This went on continuously during the first part of the winter, the weather getting worse and worse until it was too miserable to work. Men were forbidden to go outside during the worst cold spells.

We were now living in comfort and luxury compared to anything I had ever experienced before in Antarctica. There were more things to do within the confines of the base camp, more room to move around, and more opportunity for quiet if one wished to read or write or think things out alone.

There were eighteen buildings, nine on each side of the 1,000-foot tunnel that we called Main Street. They were flat-roofed with a door at each end. There were bunkhouses for our sixty-two enlisted men of all ratings, and a Battalion Officers'

Quarters in which ten of us lived. This building was divided into five cubicles that we called our rooms, with two beds in each, as well as lockers for personal gear and a small stand at the head of each bed.

These cubicles were warmed by air forced through heaters from a jet oil stove. There were rugs on the floor and curtains hung in the doorways that opened from these personal sleeping quarters into the officers' lounge, where we could write letters, play cards, talk nonsense, or discuss problems. We had electric lights to brighten the rooms, and the lounge was equipped with a table, a settee, and chairs.

In addition to the bunkhouses and officers' quarters, our community at Little America V included radio quarters, a mess hall, recreation center, powerhouse, photographic laboratory, administration building, a garage for tractors and repair, a hospital, and two communal bathrooms with heads and showers.

With movies, radio, hi-fi phonographs, a fine library, and plenty of good food, we had all the conveniences of home. The heads and washing spaces were built for comfort such as we had never known before on earlier expeditions. On our first expedition we simply dug holes out of the snow in the side of a tunnel and laid boards over the holes to serve as seats in the icy Crystal Palace, as we called it. Now a circulating fan was used to drive the heat under the floor and the seat was warm— a convenience that no Antarctic explorer in all history had ever known before.

The bunkhouses for the enlisted men were no less comfortable than the officers' quarters. Two or four men slept in each cubicle. A locker was provided for each to stow his clothes in, and there were shelves for knicknacks. The bunks were provided with blankets and clean sheets over a comfortable mattress. There was an even temperature in the rooms, which made it comfortable going to bed or getting up again. We all slept in pyjamas. And as I lay in comfort, I often thought of the built-up wooden bunks that we nailed together at Little America I, where we crawled into reindeer-skin sleeping bags at night and kept our underclothing on at all times because of the cold. We allowed the fire to go out at night to conserve fuel, and in the morning we got up in a sub-zero room with our teeth chattering.

We hardly washed at all on that first expedition. When our underwear began to stick to our bodies, we took it off and threw it away, substituting a new suit.

Now at Little America V, one day each week, a man was detailed by the hut captain to wash all the clothes for the entire group in the enlisted men's quarters. Usually he did this at night, and then had the next day off. The officers washed their clothes individually. A regular schedule was made up which came out in the plan of the day. And the washing was easy, for there were three electric washing machines set up for that purpose. We had only to run the water, put the clothes in, and push the switch. Twenty minutes later we would stop the machine, put the clothes in the rinser, and then transfer them to the drier. All we had to do then was to set the dial and forget it. When an hour was up we went back and took our clothes out, folded them up, and took them to our quarters. We put clean sheets and pillow slips on our bed and made it up. Our week's washing was done.

It was only on rare occasions that we washed even our faces on the first expedition, for water was scarce. Even though we had enough snow and ice around us to float a fleet of battleships if it were melted down, we had only a small tank to melt the snow in, and it required continual, back-breaking snow shoveling to keep it full. Now at Little America V, an eleven-ton trailer was used to haul the snow in where it was shoveled into huge melting tanks in big chunks. We could wash all we pleased. Showers were taken every day in the week, and as many times as we wished.

As total darkness settled around us, there was less activity on the part of the men on the outside. They stayed close to the shelter of the camp and worked in the heated spaces, and talked over the problems that confronted them. There were a few duties that required men to go out for a short while. The ash cans and rubbish barrels had to be taken out of the tunnels and dumped. The snow melter had to be kept filled. Fuel drums had to be brought into the tunnel. But everything possible was cached inside to save men from having to go out in the cold.

These days were cruel to men, especially those who had spent most of their lives in a temperate zone. When they did go out, they came back in again with frozen noses and faces or with features that looked red as a rooster's comb from the piercing wind, and they ran to the Sick Bay for first-aid treatment.

When I got up one morning, there was a sense of chill even in our heated cubicles. The temperature outside had dropped to 74° below zero, and the men were ordered to stay indoors.

The 1,000-foot tunnel was filled with fog, like sea smoke in the Ross Sea. Men looked like ghosts, for the vaporous atmosphere of our buried settlement's Main Street was so thick that human beings were unrecognizable, even when they drew near to you.

The electric lights at the top of the tunnel could be seen through the mist only faintly, and the lights at the further end could not be seen at all. The burlap and chicken wire which encased the tunnel had become a mat of iced beauty, glistening and sparkling in the dim lights like clusters of brilliant diamonds. The meeting of cold and warm air in the tunnel had caused the moisture to freeze into a delicate tracery which clung to the ceiling and the upper part of the walls, forming a canopy of indescribable artistry.

Outside, the blizzards screeched and howled and roared on their way to the frozen sea. Then there would come a deathlike silence and we would step outside to have a look. Sometimes there was nothing to see but the beacon light of the base, a little gleam surrounded by infinite darkness. Sometimes our eyes would be gladdened by the sight of the moon. But for all its beauty there was something deadly in this lunar revelation of Antarctica. There was no sign of life, nothing in its pale light on an endless desert of snow to break the desolation of the Barrier.

To the north was the aurora australis, gigantic and fantastic curtains of delicate colors weaving in the sky with beautiful streamers darting here and there. But we could take just so much of the universe in Antarctica, and then we would run for our shelter with its familiar ceiling and four walls, and a solid floor beneath our feet. A man is forever humbly conscious in Antarctica of both his frailty and his small size. It affects him profoundly.

In the Mess Hall, one man taps his fingers on the table for want of anything else to do. He squirms around and wriggles his feet. His nerves are on edge and he wonders what is wrong. Another man comes to chow and stabs a piece of steak with his fork. He puts it, with the gravy, on the bottom of his plate instead of turning his plate rightside up to hold it. The gravy runs down on the table. He stares at it. Then he roars with laughter. Another man comes in and does the same thing. He too stares for a moment at what he has done. He shakes his head and swears a little.

The men sought relief from this puzzling state by gathering together and talking of familiar things which concerned them personally. We all became good listeners in this commonly-shared need for talk. Around each table in the Mess Hall a different subject was being thrashed out and argued over. Many of these subjects were of interest only from the speaker's point of view, but I never saw the other men show any impatience.

One man would tell about the funny dream he had had the night before; another would talk about his next duty assignment; and still another about his liberty in New Zealand. New cars and old ones were hot subjects.

The men all seemed to want shore duty in a nice secluded spot where it was warm and where there were lots of people. They wanted to see new faces and new surroundings, and not this desolation and isolation of snow and ice. A few talked about retirement and a little place where they could settle down, to call their own. But the undercurrent to all this kind of talk was the thought, expressed or unexpressed, of a woman—wife, sweetheart, or dream as the case might be.

There was universal sympathy for the heart affair of any man amongst us. We all watched one boy anxiously, as he paced back and forth like a man walking in his sleep—eyes open, yet seeing none of us. In any other environment he might have been kidded unmercifully, but not in Antarctica. He had received a radio message from his best girl, telling him she was going to be married to another man.

I felt particularly sympathetic because I had just talked to Ada by radio telephone for half an hour. It is really something to be at the bottom of the world during a long Antarctic night and then suddenly find yourself talking with your wife more than nine thousand miles away in Grand Rapids, Michigan.

No one could understand what the sound of her voice meant to me unless he, too, had wintered-over through the long, dark nights of earlier expeditions when we hung around the radio waiting for a chance to send a brief message. Since I dug my

first shovelful of snow on the great ice Barrier and felt the
first prickles in my scalp from the awesome noises and overwhelming silences of this desolate continent, I had never before
talked from here with a loved one at home. Today this is a
common experience for men on the frozen continent. The geographic distance has not lessened, but the psychological distance
has because science has conquered both space and time.

But the Antarctic night is just as dark and lonely and cold
as it ever was, for all the advancements of modern science. We
were cut off from civilization, save by radio, in the most awesome darkness on earth; and not one of us could forget it for
a single moment. It was a psychological ordeal for everyone, in
spite of all the provisions that had been made for our comfort,
mental diversion, and morale. Four months is a long night to be
cooped up within four walls, any way you look at it.

There are nights when you cannot sleep. You are in agony,
and you cannot explain why. You can't seem to find a comfortable position. You close your eyes and try to forget your
thoughts of home and loved ones. But sleep will not come, so
you twist and turn again on the other side.

You wonder if morning will ever come. You know you cannot tell by the daylight, because there isn't any. You look at
the watch on your wrist for the time, but the dial doesn't seem
to glow any more. Your eyes are foggy and you are not sure
which is the long or short hand. So you switch on the light above
your head and see that it is only a little past midnight. You
pick up the book you have been reading, but you are not sure
of the right page. You forgot to mark it, but it does not matter;
you have forgotten what the story was about. You start at the
beginning again. There is a plaguing awareness of the appalling
magnitude of your isolation which makes it difficult to concentrate. It makes a story seem contrived and unimportant, but

you force yourself to read anyway because it keeps your mind from going too far astray.

Your eyelids finally begin to droop, and the book falls out of your hands, and you stay that way until your shoulders begin to feel cold. Then you turn off the light, squirm down under the covers and drift off to sleep . . . but not for long. You awaken suddenly with a feeling of fright.

You heard a bell ringing, and now you listen to its echo in your memory, trying to identify it. Yes, you are sure it was a bell. But where did it come from? Its echo sounds like the ringing of a cowbell on a farm. Reassured, you drift off and hear it again, this time ringing soft and clear like the chimes from the tower of an old village church. You lie there and listen to the ringing. It is music to your ears and your body relaxes. But suddenly it stops and you come to your senses, disappointed. For a little while you had forgotten you were in another world where you cannot join the congregation in fellowship singing of sacred hymns. Perhaps you seldom or never did this in civilization, but you think of it now.

It is a common experience in the enforced solitude of an Antarctic night to hear peculiar sounds. Some of these have a local origin in the howling of a blizzard outside or the groaning and cracking of the Barrier ice. But many of my own experiences have been of psychological origin, reminiscent of the hustle and bustle of civilization; and these are not "dreams" in the ordinary sense. I have heard them often in the waking or half-waking state. Perhaps they are the mind's subconscious reaction to a silence prolonged beyond its capacity of endurance, like the illusion of the eyes when they see things in empty space or the ears when they hear a roaring in a noiseless atmosphere.

Often as I lay in bed I thought I heard a whistle which one time sounded like a ship's horn screeching out a warning in a fog, and another time like a factory whistle. Then I would think I was home again, listening to all the noises of a crowded city. I would hear brakes screeching on cars, horns blowing to warn pedestrians, gears meshing and grinding in the rising whine of a take-off. With these sounds in my inner ears I could fall asleep. Then when I woke up it would take a little while to adjust myself. I was buried under drifting snow, surrounded by inky blackness, at the bottom of the world; and it would be a long while before I heard the sounds of civilization again.

6

SCARCELY anyone answered to his real name during our long confinement in the Antarctic night. One by one nicknames were born to fit the men, and not one got sore or hurt about it. Everyone laughed it off in respect to the unwritten rule of sportsmanship that has governed every expedition of my experience. It is the same with practical jokes. Everything is laughed off in good humor. The spirit of retaliation is entirely absent in Antarctica.

One of the supply men was called "Pencil" because he carried one back of his ear all the time. Another was called "Ugly" because he had grown a beard.

"Mother" was adopted as the name of one of the hut captains because he was in charge of all the enlisted men in that dwelling. His job was to look out for them and take care of their wants like a house mother in college.

"Goblet" was the smallest man in camp, weighing 125 pounds. Our favorite delight was to watch him boxing with Big Ed, who weighed over two hundred pounds and stood over six feet.

It was the movies, however, which provided us with the greatest enjoyment. Pictures were shown every day and twice on Saturdays. They were the most effective escape that could have been devised to give men respite from exile. For a little while we felt almost as if we were home, and living again.

It has been said that celibacy enforced by absolute isolation is no real problem in this coldest and most desolate place on earth. Admiral Byrd is quoted as having said, "The greatest lack in the Antarctic is the lack of temptation." But a man's separation from his wife and family, if he truly loves them, is the source of his greatest suffering during the long Antarctic night when he has no work and adventure and danger to distract him.

I am sure that not a day went by without our thinking of the opposite sex. Of all the world we had left behind us, they alone commanded our continuous interest because they were a part of us, and here in Antarctica there is universal sympathy and respect for the lonely longing and devotion of every man for his wife or sweetheart.

The days and nights went by as we counted them off, waiting for the return of the sun; and during this time I had my own private anticipation. As the only Antarctic veteran among us, I wanted to see its effect on the other men. Would it affect them as it had every last man of us on previous expeditions? I was not disappointed.

When word passed through the camp that the sun could be seen again, every man, including me, rushed out of doors. Only a few took time out to put on extra clothing. Men ran in every direction but the right one toward the entrance to the tunnel. Almost in a daze they looked around for the highest mounds of snow they could find, where no object would obliterate the view they had waited so long to see. Some ascended the observation tower, others walked on the roofs of the huts, still others climbed poles and clambered up on top of tractors, slipping on the ice-coated metal, burning their hands on the stinging surface in their haste to see the first faint light in the northern sky.

At first there was only a red dot on the black "water sky" over the Ross Sea; then slowly it rose like a flaming red ball of fire and the camp came to life in hoarse cheers.

In a short while all was dark again, but Little America V was reborn. All was bustle in preparation and anticipation of the ceremonies which would take place on the day the full solar orb appeared above the horizon. The raising of the flag again would mark the turning of the black tide of darkness.

At 10:30 A.M. on August 20 the men were mustered near the flagpole. We faced the south, with a cold wind blowing into our faces at 42° below zero. We were all so bundled up in warm clothing, with hoods over our heads and faces, that it was impossible to tell one man from another.

The sun was just showing above the rim of the Barrier to the north, through a foggy mist that filtered out all rays but those of a cold red ball.

"At-ten-tion!"

The color guard was ready. One man held the flag, another held the halyards, and two others stood at attention, facing the flagpole. Then came the order to salute, and the colors were smartly hoisted to the top of the mast.

The men were quickly dismissed, and we all ran for shelter. The tide had turned, but it was still dark and miserable. Although very little work could be done out of doors, the Plan of the Day called for a change back to working routine. Reveille sounded at 5:00 A.M. with breakfast at 5:30 and turn-to at 6:30. We had a big schedule before us. Everything on the outside was buried underneath the snow and had to be dug out again.

During the next two months we seemed to be fighting a losing game. Equipment was dug up and snaked out of the snow by the tractors, only to have another blizzard come down and cover it up again. Only one or two tractors could be kept running every day, for in the low temperatures they broke down or froze up. The rubber tracks on the weasel snapped, and it took many hours to repair them. The men could stay outside for only a short time before their hands and feet and faces were frozen. More than fifty cases of frostbite occurred almost immediately. Men were continually running for shelter and the Sick Bay to thaw out.

Dr. Ehrlich and his assistants were kept busy. Not only frostbite but sore backs, cut fingers, and innumerable aches and pains required immediate diagnosis and treatment. One man was operated on for appendicitis. Doc even made up a concoction for hair tonic that was used for dry scalps. He passed out vitamin capsules by the hundreds.

The sun came up a little higher each day, and often the horizon was illuminated with a crimson glow of light that sent rays almost to the zenith. The vivid colors dispelled the gloom of loneliness. Men became cheerful and smiled as they went out to do their work; but the cheer was not as deep as the cold in their bones and the time-exposure of the long Antarctic night. The feeling of adventure had left them entirely. It was all just gruelling work. But the motto of the Seabees is *Can do,* and they lived up to it. No job was too great for them to tackle; no task too difficult for them to accomplish. They were well picked, these men; my hat is off to them all in memories never to be forgotten.

The sun crossed the line on the twenty-first of September, and every man in camp looked forward to it. There was nothing to see that was different from the day before, but it meant that the sun was coming our way again, into the Southern Hemisphere. And as the days passed, the effect of this became noticeable. We began to screw up our faces and squint our eyes when we went outside during midday. Shadows began to form from big drifts of snow, and as the sun got stronger and brighter a little warmth was felt from its rays.

The month of September was still cold, and many of the men continued to wear masks to protect their faces. But warm or cold, strong wind or calm, there was one man who always wore his mask with just his eyes showing. He was soon christened "Tender Face," but you could hardly blame him for this caution because the cap he wore was a small protection against the wintry cold.

October came in with the good news that the planes were on their way to us. We got word that they would take off from New Zealand for McMurdo Sound on October 15, and then fly on to Little America. The U.S.S. *Glacier* had also left the United States for the Antarctic. The whole camp came to life again with this stimulant. We knew that the planes were bringing our first mail. It is impossible to describe the anticipation with which we looked forward to those letters from our friends and loved ones.

The sun was now rising higher and ever higher and the temperature began to go up. The glare of the sun on the ice was terrific; we could not look to the north without shading our eyes, and we were forced to begin wearing snow glasses.

The shoreline of the Barrier was a riot of colors in the slanting rays of the returning sun. Leaving camp one day, Willis Clem, Lloyd Beebe, and I skied down over the first snow hill to the valley of crevasses. New hummocks revealed bad places to be wary of. The big crevasse which had been bridged for the tractors the year before was filled up with snow. There was now little difficulty in crossing it on skis.

Most of the flagstaffs that marked the trail were still standing, but the flags themselves were either frayed out or blown clean from the staff.

The next snow hill was much steeper, difficult to climb with our skis. We were short-winded from so little exercise during the long night, and we had to stop for breath before we reached the top.

From there it was easy going out over the ridge to the end of the Barrier where the mighty *Glacier* had been tied up before she left us in March. She would have to break out the ice again, or we would have to go out over the bay ice to meet her. Would the bay ice support the tractors for unloading? I decided to find out.

There was only one place where we could get down to the bay ice, and that was on a snow ramp that had drifted into the form of a whale's back, with a few sastrugi stretched across the hump. They could be seen only faintly in the foglike mist that hung over the surface. All was sheer whiteness to the eyes, and the crisscrossed ridges forced us to go slowly as we picked our way over them.

On the bay ice itself there was little snow, for most of it had been blown out into the Ross Sea. I took off my skis to rest my feet, and walked . . . but only for a few steps. I began to sink into a large crack in the newly frozen ice. It was filled with soft snow, and beneath it were many fathoms of icy sea. As I was going down, I caught myself by falling lengthwise at right angles to the crack. After that I put my skis back on again.

Far out over the ice to the north could be seen sea smoke, which signaled the presence of patches of open water along the edge. The bay was frozen in line with the two capes that formed Kainan Bay. Sharp, perpendicular walls formed the shore line on two sides, while the head of the bay was a mass of broken and twisted ice. Huge blocks of ice had been heaved up by the great pressure, and I could almost hear the echo of the tumult they must have raised.

But Kainan Bay was quiet now. The heaved-up blocks were silent as ghosts, appearing and disappearing in the white, shifting mist. When the sun broke through the clouds, they turned into glistening ramparts and castles, large and bold.

We proceeded carefully, probing with an iron rod. Part way out in the bay we began cutting a hole in the ice with an ax. This was slow work, but we decided it was the only way to find out how thick the ice really was. Others had tried dynamite and burning with gasoline, which had proved useless.

After hours of hacking and probing with ax and rod, we were down only seven feet and decided not to go any further. It was solid blue ice, and very hard. We figured it must be ten feet thick, at least, and strong enough to hold the tractors when the ships came in. But that was another two months away.

Meanwhile, the planes were on our minds. For the first time in Antarctic history, mail would reach us before the ships could get down and in to us.

The first plane, an R5D, took off from New Zealand on October 16, with Admiral Dufek aboard. It landed safely at Mc-Murdo Sound on the morning of the seventeenth. This was great news to all the men at Little America V. The mail and new faces were only a little more than four hundred miles away from us.

Six other planes were in readiness for the take-off and soon followed. But they had a rough trip from New Zealand before they landed on the McMurdo Bay ice, and their arrival was shrouded in the gloom of tragedy. The leading plane landed short of the runway in a crash landing, and the pilot and three of the crew were killed.

On October 22 we received word that the R4D's would take off from McMurdo Sound to bring us our mail. It was the uppermost thought in the mind of every man at Little America Station.

Everything was made ready for the arrival of the planes. The working parties with their tractors and sleds stood by and were told what to do. The photographers had their cameras all set to shoot. The official welcoming party with the weasels and sno-cats had everything under control; we were ready to roll at an instant's notice.

But nothing happened. After waiting for hours, we finally received word that the planes would not come because of necessary maintenance work on the engines.

This was a big disappointment. Every one of us had thought surely we would get our mail that evening. There was nothing in Antarctica, no event on the whole earth, so important to us as this.

The next day came and went . . . we were still waiting. We thought that they had forgotten us. The men talked of nothing else. The party at McMurdo Sound had not only received their mail, but their outgoing mail had already gone to New Zealand and was well on its way to the United States.

The morning of the twenty-fourth was dazzling in its beauty. The temperature was 26° below zero, but there was no wind. The skies above were clear and the sun was blazing in a blue sky. Visibility was unlimited, and we were sure that we would receive the mail. No one could ask for a better day.

Word came that the plane had taken off and was on its way to Little America V. Our hopes soared again, but they were soon shattered by a report that the plane was headed for the Beardmore Glacier, and beyond to the Queen Maud Range.

Morale took a drop. Men walked back and forth with long faces. There was no word from McMurdo about mail or the departure of the plane for Little America. Now that McMurdo men had received their mail, they apparently weren't interested in us.

We read a press story that a reporter had sent from McMurdo Sound to the United States. It said that the mail was being flown to the seventy-two men who had wintered-over at Little America V. The story was two days old when it reached us. Conversation started to buzz about the mail back home.

One man said, "My wife will call up John Doe's wife and she will brag about the mail she just received from her husband. Then what will my wife say? That she never received a word from me."

"My wife will get a divorce," said another, "if she finds out that other women are getting mail from down here, and she thinks I haven't written her."

Work came almost to a standstill. The men had no ambition or desire to do anything. When they came in for coffee or tea, they would sit, brooding and silent, until someone broke the spell by mentioning the mail. Then their tongues would wag like the clapper of a bell.

Eight months was a long time to go without mail, and more than a week's delay in delivering it from McMurdo Sound only four hundred miles away seemed a cruel torture to the men at Little America V.

The twenty-fifth was another beautiful day. At three o'clock in the morning it was 30° below. The visibility was good, and it remained so all day. Word came in that the R4D had arrived back at McMurdo from her flight to the glacier. But there was no word about a plane coming to Little America.

The day dragged on in silence, with little or no heart for work. At intervals men went outside to observe the weather. It became a habit for everyone to go out and gaze steadily up into the sky.

At 5:00 P.M. a cry went up that the plane had left for Little America with the mail. No one would believe it. We had all heard that cry too often. One man voiced the mood of all: "I will believe it when I see her landing."

But rumor spread that it was true. She wasn't due for over

three hours, but men went out to scan the sky, still hardly believing the report.

Word was received then that she would arrive at 9:00 P.M., but the hour came and went with no signs of a plane. "I knew she wasn't coming," said some.

But the sno-cats, weasels, and tractor had already left for Kiel Field to be on hand for the welcome, and to bring the mail in.

Orders came over the P.A. system that no man would be allowed near the field when the plane landed except those whose names were called out. Everyone listened, and those whose names were not called started muttering. Orders were orders, and they had to be obeyed, but they did not set very well with men who had waited many months for the first plane to come in.

Men stood for hours on top of the roofs of the huts and on the observation tower to spot the plane coming in and to get a picture of her if possible. I walked part way out on the trail and at 9:45 P.M. saw her flying east toward the runway. The men, almost frozen stiff waiting for her, came to life and roared a welcome.

7

NO one else can know what that night meant to us. There was mail for everyone, and not as we know it at home, but many months' accumulation of it.

One man was dazed when he was handed five hundred letters from his wife. Another staggered away with part of a bag full, all for him.

And I had my share, too, more than I had ever received before at one time. Besides all the letters from my wife and daughter, relatives and friends, one school had the whole class write me letters asking all sorts of questions. A boy from Missouri wanted to know all about the Antarctic. It would take me a long time to answer them all, but I would be happy doing it.

None of us slept that night, for we were all reading letters and clippings, looking at snapshots, and reading over and over again those special letters nearest to the heart from those we loved.

We were happy men. We were not forgotten. The long over-due mail had come through. And now we could work again—carrying on with what we had come to do when the Antarctic night was over.

But I was still in a daze myself, like a man with his feet glued to a rug. Throughout the months of darkness I had been writing down the story of my experiences on this and previous expeditions, trying to show why I loved Antarctica in spite of all I had endured at her hands, and why a man should ever want to return again and again to this most lonely, alluring, and forbidding of ice-locked lands. Now the long overdue mail had brought the actual contract for this book about it. I was asked to pack up everything I had written, and ship it out by air as soon as possible. . . .

So here it is, and I hope it will convey some understanding of what Antarctic exploration means—not to science, but to the men who have endured the rigors of its trail blazing and the loneliness of the long Antarctic night.

As long as we live, there is not a man of us who will ever forget his shipmates at Little America V. It is not quite the same where the numbers are greater and the hardships less; and there is no denying that civilization has invaded Antarctica, with greater comfort. Mechanized transport has changed the entire character of exploration today; both trail blazing and transport are no longer "adventure," they are just jobs. But Antarctica is eternal and her spirit is all-pervading; she subdues the mind and penetrates the very bones of men to mark them for life and set them apart from other men. They have this forever in common: that in their very souls they bear the seal of Antarctica; they can never more be the same. And to each comes the same Commendation:

FROM: Commander Task Force Forty-Three
To: Lt. Cdr. Jacob J. Bursey, U.S.C.G.R., 36196
VIA: (1) Commander, U.S. Naval Bases, Antarctica
      (2) Officer in Charge, Little America V, Antarctica
SUBJECT: Letter of Commendation
   1. From November 1955 to March 1957 you were a member of the wintering-over group that successfully constructed from the ground up, Little America V at Kainan Bay, Antarctica. During this

period your competence, integrity, moral courage, ruggedness and untiring efforts contributed materially to the success of Operation Deepfreeze.

2. Under the most adverse conditions, in complete isolation and subjected to frequent blizzards and sub-zero temperature during a four-month continuous Antarctic Night, your personal achievements and sacrifices were in keeping with the highest traditions of the U.S. Navy. Well done.

GEORGE DUFEK

The "old days" of a primitive adventure are gone forever in Antarctica, but the memory does not dim with the passing years. I can still see the faces of the men who were with me, looking just as they did out on the trail as we sledged the cold and weary miles with our dogs and camped with the blizzards howling about us, rattling the sides of our little tents.

Arthur Walden's face is before me as I write this, wrinkled in places from the toil and sweat, the killing cold, and the long hours without rest. At sixty-two years of age, his features were weatherbeaten from a life following the Yukon trails up in Alaska. His eyes had a gleam and a twinkle in them that made his expression both gentle and interesting. He knew dogs well, and had as fine a team of Chinooks as was ever put in harness; and when his splendid old lead-dog, Chinook, wandered off and never came back again we all felt his sorrow with him because we knew that he had wanted so much to bury Chinook in his harness.

I can see the face of Chris Braathen, the Norwegian who came out with the *Samson* from Norway, with a broad smile that crinkled up his eyes and showed a row of strong upper teeth. We became friends at first sight, little dreaming that together we were to encounter the most dangerous crevasse area in Antarctica.

Joe de Ganahl was the fourth member of that sledging trip in support of the South Polar flight on Admiral Byrd's first expedition. He was younger than Chris and Arthur, but older than I and from a different sphere of life. He was just one of us, like all the rest, and we got along together well. He was a dependable trail mate and his fine, boyish face, courage, and enthusiasm balanced the more rugged features and characters of our two older companions.

I am the only survivor, after twenty-eight years, of that historic trail-blazing trip to the Queen Maud Range, when St. Lunaire led my team and all of us safely through the dangerous crevasse area which threatened to block our passage. When I recall the flap-eared mongrel husky from Labrador that I fell in love with, and how proudly he carried his plumed tail up over his back in undisputed leadership, I find the whole spirit of that adventurous era of "man and dogs against the ice" immortalized in his memory. His intelligent, questioning eyes and keen ears ever attuned to my voice exemplified the kind of partnership which made Antarctic exploration possible.

With the finest of dogs as partners and the finest of men as companions on the trail, my boyhood dreams found fulfillment; life held no higher adventure than sledging in the midnight sun or camping in the world's worst blizzards, pushing on, ever on, into the icy Unknown of the most tantalizing and bewitching land on earth, a once-tropical land that had been buried for fifty thousand years or more beneath an ice age which hides from man the mysteries of Antarctica.

Never shall I forget the face of Admiral, then Commander, Byrd with its concern for our safety as we set forth, its happy relief when we returned and its tired but radiant smile when he climbed out of the plane after his successful flight to the South Pole. He, too, recalled these things and spoke of them to me twenty-seven years later as we stood atop sixty feet of snow over our buried camp at Little America I, as I raised the flag and planted it there for the last time. We were two of the little group who had first learned to love Antarctica together. No hardships of the passing years and further expeditions, no bitter cold wind, no raving blizzard, no weary hours, not even the long and lonely Antarctic nights on the desolate Barrier had power to obliterate or even dim the memories of that first Great Adventure in the Great White South.

There were only three of us on the 1,220-mile sledging trip to Hal Flood Mountain which climaxed the "man and dog" era of Antarctic exploration in 1940. With our eighteen dogs we came to grips with Antarctica in all her moods, but none could eclipse the awesome magnitude and unearthly beauty of this loneliest land on earth in her benign and sunlit moments. They were worth all the months of hardship we had to pay for them. Dick Moulton, Leonard Berlin, and I found more in Antarctica than the mountains we set out to survey and the lonely peaks which bear our names. We found and sensed the sleeping spirit of a lost world which engulfed us in emotions that defy the use of words as a medium of expression; and such unexpressed and un-expressible emotions brew a strange kind of love which preserves all the memories of their origin.

I have only seen Dick once since we returned in 1941, and Leonard not at all. But as long as we are living there is a bond between us—a bond as immune to time as the glaciated moun-tains which served as our goal in united endeavor. Antarctica initiates men into her own secret fraternity and gives birth to friendships unlike any that civilization knows. Should we meet again in the years to come, it will be like a reunion of long-lost brothers.

And as my crew of Seabees and I battled the crevasses on our way to the mountains with sno-cats and a weasel in 1956, and as I looked down upon the great Ross Barrier, the continental plateau, and the familiar peaks of distant mountain ranges in our reconnaissance flights, the memories of former years passed through my mind in review. Antarctica is the same as she ever was, and still she is not the same to men who attack her in greater numbers with mechanized weapons. No man flying a plane or driving a tractor train into the interior of this frozen continent can ever know the Antarctica we knew in days of old when we traveled on foot and skis behind a team of wonderful dogs.

When I think of my big Eskimo husky lead dog, King, and my little Siberian beauty, Gray Cloud, and all the rest of the faithful dogs who gave all they had in loyalty and strength that we might reach our goal and return again, I feel the essence of an era with its secret: The mind of man is overwhelmed by the immensity of the Universe and of God as revealed in the appalling isolation and bewitching beauty of sleeping Antarctica; but in the love and dependency between man and dogs these immensities are somehow brought into focus.

After 28,224 hours at the bottom of the world my love for the land that some men fear and hate has remained steadfast. It was born in the love of a boy for his dogs on the winter icebound coast of northern Newfoundland. It matured in the love of a man for his dogs when his life depended on them out on the trail in Antarctica. Love . . . adventure . . . mystery . . . beauty . . . hardship . . . hazard . . . Mix all these ingredients well in the Midnight Sun and deepfreeze them through three long Antarctic nights; then thaw them out in the warm memories of lifelong friendships with the finest men on earth, and you have the eternal spirit of Antarctica resurrected in your heart. You cannot help but love her even though she might one day kill you.